May you abide in christ.
Nina Looke
2017

Nina Spencer Locke

# Twice

# Chosen

*A Story of Reunion and Redemption*

By Nina Spencer Locke

Nina Spencer Locke

"*I am the vine: you are the branches. If a man remains in me and I in him, he will bear much fruit, apart from me you can do nothing....This is to my Father's glory, that you bear much fruit, showing yourselves to be my disciples*"

(John 15, 5, 8).

The Scripture in this book comes from the following versions of the Bible: New International Version NIV); New American Standard Bible (NASB); Authorized (King James) Version (AKJV); Living Bible (TLB); English Standard Version (ESV); New King James Version (NKJV); and the New Living Translation (NLT).

Cover photos by Dede Locke Smith, www.photogirl.us.

Photo of Lisa Caracciolo Rosselini pg 147 (used by permission) by Marcellino Radogna

Published by EA Books Publishing a division of
Living Parables of Central Florida, Inc. a 501c3
eabookspublishing.com

# DEDICATION

*Dedicated to my dear husband Jim, who continually encouraged me to take this journey.*

*To our three children, who supported me in the writing of a family history and to the generations who follow.*

*May they come to know the unlimited goodness of God's grace and His Providence.*

# ACKNOWLEDGMENTS

My heart is full of gratitude to the people who prayed and helped make this book possible:

I owe much to Vicki Buchhold who built a story line from my numerous journals and files. Without her research and writing skills, this book would not have been written.

To my daughter Dede, for her enumerable dedicated hours of computer work and photographic expertise. She went the extra mile.

I thank those who came alongside me and modeled the Spirit filled life.

Nina Spencer Locke

# 1

# Choosing Denia

*January 26, 1980*

The plane ascended over familiar highways, cityscapes, and even over my own Winter Park home. Lakes and groves created a colorful pattern across Central Florida, which quickly became fading dots spattered upon the distant ground. My anticipation surged.

I had made this trip to New York City numerous times. The city held fond memories and pieces of my heart. However this time I didn't travel to revisit the familiar footsteps of my childhood, or my family. I went to meet a sister I had never known.

I had been told it would be impossible with the little information that I had uncovered. I wasn't deterred. I said,

"I know the God of the impossible and if He wants me to find her, He can bring it about." The search had taken two years. Barbara had been found and I was on my way to see her face to face. *What would she be like? What would we think of each other?* How many small events had worked together to lead to this meeting, to direct my steps along this path?

The doors were beginning to open and show me how God had orchestrated my life. The story began long before my search for a long-lost sister. The journey had woven through generations of hope, loss, and answered prayers, to bring me to this day. It was the providence of God—He directs all things seen and unseen by the Word of His power.

*"I know the plans I have for you, declares the Lord, plans to prosper you and not to harm you, plans to give you hope and a future"* (Jeremiah 29:11).

I unbuckled my seatbelt and tried to relax. I had known since childhood that I was adopted and had a younger sister. My roots had grown deep in places far from that of my origin. The Spencer's assured me that they had chosen me. I had two brothers, but  what would it be like to have a real sister?

I became a Spencer at twenty-two months. I was the daughter of a woman who, after abandoning me, would walk away from three more children. Moragh MacColl, my birth mother, was nineteen and unmarried. My grandmother was Ethel Chase MacColl—known to friends as "Chasey." They named me "Denia" after the fragrant gardenia flower. After my birth in New York City, Moragh remained in the hospital because of phlebitis. The doctor determined that it would not be good for me to remain there, so I went home with Chasey. Her love for me was deep, but as an artist, her life was ill-suited to raising another generation.

Moragh and Chasey's stories were part of who I am. Growing up, I didn't need to know about my past. "You were chosen, and that makes you special" my new mother said. The Spencer's provided for me in ways I would never have known if they hadn't made me theirs. They were not perfect, but they were parents I adored.

Marjorie Thorp and C.B. Spencer met in New York. He was a dashing bachelor about town. She was the shy type, newly planted in Manhattan, having come from Minnesota to share an apartment with her single girlfriends. C.B. swept her off her feet.

They married and had a good life with their two boys, Burr and Bill. After a few years they became discontent and spoke of divorce. Hoping their problems could be resolved; C.B. suggested that Marjorie take a trip to think things over. She was to travel by train to California and then by ship to Hawaii. That first night on the train she realized she couldn't leave her boys. She made one request of her husband: If they reconciled, could they adopt a little girl? C.B. consented and Marjorie returned home.

In Riverdale, a Hudson River suburb of New York, the Spencer's stone house sat high on a hill overlooking a pond. Large oaks, manicured green lawns, forsythia, and rhododendrons bloomed amidst huge rock outcroppings.

One day in 1931, Marjorie welcomed a group of ladies for tea. Helen Molitor was a guest from Maine. Marjorie told her friends that she had visited adoption agencies in search of a little girl. In her own witty way she said, "But I haven't found one I like." Helen mentioned that her cousin Chasey had been caring for her granddaughter Denia, but was now seeking an adoptive family. It was a providential conversation that would play an important part of God's unfolding plan for me.

**Chasey**

The Spencer's and Chasey arranged a six-week stay for me in Riverdale. When our trial time ended, adoption proceedings were fulfilled. For my grandmother, parting with me was a heart-wrenching decision. Denia would now belong to someone else. My life in the MacColl clan ended and at 22 months, new life as a Spencer began.

2

## Nina Stanley Spencer

I was given a new name and a new birthday. Mommy changed the date from November 13th to the 11th to match her own mother's birthday — my new grandmother Vivian. At eighteen, when I applied for my driver's license, I discovered that I was two days younger than I thought!

As the flight to New York continued, memories flooded my mind. My father, Charles Burr Spencer, was six foot four, with reddish brown hair and blue eyes. He was an imposing figure, strong and lean, handsome in a rugged way. I loved his confident gait as he walked, swinging a cane much in the debonair manner of the French actor, Maurice Chevalier. Men admired him and women adored him. In a word, he was charming.

**C.B. Spencer**

He wore three-piece tweed suits and donned a felt hat. Nestled in one vest pocket was a watch on a gold chain, a tiny gold knife and file in the other pocket. On the chain between, hung his Columbia University honor key, his engineer's medal, and the Engineering Society medal. Years later, these small treasures became mine.

A civil engineer with an international reputation...his company did foundation work for the NYC subway system, skyscrapers, tunnels, bridges, dry docks, and moved huge buildings. To be consulted on a project like the Tower of Pisa was a great honor. In 1947 his company was selected to do all the foundation work for the restoration of the White House under the Truman administration. He developed the "drilled-in caisson" process for unstable foundations. Challenging jobs that others thought were too difficult was what he liked.

C.B. had a fabulous sense of humor, telling stories and jokes in many dialects. Often his written letters flowed into poetry and his presents always came with a limerick. He had a particular whistle and call for me after coming home from work. His created nickname was: "Where's my little bit of a sawed off, hammered down, knock-kneed, pigeon-toed, cross eyed, duck footed, wall-eyed okay-toot?" He loved life and lived it to the fullest. My Daddy was the light of my life.

My mother was a petite woman, a foot shorter than Daddy, with brown hair, brown eyes, and a warm smile. She had a quick wit and often turned awkward or mundane moments into humorous events. Warm, generous, and friendly, she had many friends from all walks of life, and compassion for those in need.

**Marjorie Spencer**

Mommy had exquisite taste in clothes and décor. She loved the arts: classical music, theater, poetry, literature, and opera. As I went along with her, I grew to love them also. She recognized my creative abilities at an early age and helped me develop my talents.

Her hands were always busy, creating beautiful embroidered patchwork lap robes from designer fabric samples, backed with red velvet. She taught me to sew, knit, paint, and we often read book selections that later became classics. *Charlotte's Web*, *Stuart Little*, and *Violet* were familiar to me long before they became widely appreciated. We read *The Child's Garden of Verses* over and over, particularly *The Land of Counterpane* and *The Lamplighter*.

Mommy made our home comfortable and inviting. Always a gracious hostess, she was anxious about her role, doubting that she had measured up. Apologizing when there was no reason to do so. My brother Bill later described her as "a little, wounded bird."

I too was wounded and extremely insecure. Mommy in her affectionate way tried to draw me out of my shell, but my childhood was one of painful shyness, self-consciousness, fear of making a mistake or being thought of as dumb. I came into a strong, intelligent, but critical family and I was often intimidated by my brothers.

I imagine Burr and Bill were not too enthusiastic when my parents brought home a toddler and said, "Meet your new sister." Over the years I loved, looked up to, and admired them both.

**Bill, Al Commet,
and Burr**

3

## Life in Riverdale

The hand of God took a little girl from a questionable background and grafted her into the Spencer family. I lived in their beautiful home in Fieldston, a part of Riverdale.

The house was built in 1929, during the Great Depression. Jules Gregory, the architect, had gained recognition for his French chateau-style houses. The white-washed stone and Irish slate roof made a gracious picture. On the day of completion, Daddy sold his last shares of John Deere stock and the market crashed the following day.

They gave me a lovely suite on the third floor. The bedroom was flanked by four dormer windows overlooking the pond and the pool. I wanted "real" leaded windows like those throughout the rest of the house. An arched fireplace at the end of the room gave it a cozy atmosphere.

The pool was carved out of the natural rock. In spring, blossoms of rhododendrons reflected in the shimmering water. My Daddy's greatest pleasure after work in the city was to float on his back and say, "This is the life, men!"

The pool didn't have a filter, so he partially drained it and then siphoned out the remaining water with a hose. I watched him use this same principle in his wine cellar moving wine from bottle to bottle using a little red rubber tube. Before Prohibition began, he purchased many wines and liquors.

The third floor also housed the servants. We had two German servants: Mary Pineult the maid, and Mia Kapinski the cook. Mary was so short that my brothers nicknamed her "Mary Peanut." I remember Mia most for preparing party appetizers; she would slather a whole piece of bread with Russian caviar and then cut out different designs. I learned

to love caviar as I gobbled up the trimmings.

My lovely "nursemaid," Rose Chapman, was a beautiful fair-skinned black woman with a gorgeous smile, resembling Lena

Horne. She came from Goldsboro, North Carolina, where her father had a sulky (two-wheeled cart) racetrack with a hundred horses. Rose went to an Episcopal school in Raleigh, but was raised in a Baptist church. She may have been the first believer placed in my life to pray for me. Rose left when I went to boarding school but visited occasionally. In 1950, she helped me dress on my wedding day and we kept in touch until her death at age ninety-two.

My mind snapped back to the present as I looked out the tiny window. The jet was soaring too high for me to see what was below as we flew in and out of wispy white clouds. The flight attendant asked if I would like something to drink. "No thank you," I said, as I heard my brother Bill's voice echoing, "Mary Peanut."

Bill was outgoing, popular, and a natural comedian. His stuttering didn't slow him down. He was the outdoor kind, athletic, physically strong, and a risk taker. But it was Burr who as I grew, tried to teach me how to catch a ball, play golf, and "whatever you do, don't run like a girl."

My brothers often teased me about my big ears and to this day I won't get a haircut that reveals them. Burr also zeroed in on my boney knees. "Patellas," he called them. At least I learned the correct terminology.

The boys loved tormenting me with *The Book of Monsters*. It was full of spider pictures magnified a hundred times! They held my head still and made me look at the photos. If I closed my eyes, they would pry them open. One spider had a row of eight eyes across the top his head! The more I screamed, the more delighted my brothers became!

There was also a senior member of our family, Grandpa Spencer. He was a retired physician, but I recall him as a toothless old gentleman gumming his food at holiday dinners. He pinched the maids and before the meal ended he would suddenly stand and recite *all* verses of "The Village Blacksmith" by Longfellow:

> *Under a spreading chestnut-tree*
> *The village smithy stands;*
> *The smith, a mighty man is he,*
> *With large and sinewy hands;*
> *And the muscles of his brawny arms*
> *Are strong as iron bands. etc.*

Mommy told me that Grandpa Spencer never accepted me because he didn't approve of adoption. He was distant and referred to me as "the little girl who lives in your house whose name I cannot recall."

We all anticipated Daddy's preparatory ceremony to carve the Thanksgiving turkey. He stood erect at the end of the long table and with great gusto, and the clashing noise of metal on metal, his knives flew back and forth over the stone. Our holiday favorites were creamed onions, stuffing, and mince pie with hard sauce. We alternated the annual Thanksgiving dinner with Uncle Ed and Aunt Kitty in their Ossining home. Ed was Daddy's brother, who made me very uncomfortable because I didn't know how to respond to his satirical teasing. His wife, Kitty, was so kind and the most gracious hostess. A turkey would be placed at the table, a number of pieces carved, then it was removed and another one put in its place. At the other end of the table stood a standing roast of beef! Kitty's guest rooms were always supplied with every need a guest might have. As an adult, I followed her example in our guest room. After the holiday dinner, we would each find a chair, sofa, or hammock on the porch, and nap the afternoon away.

At Christmas, in Riverdale, a tall tree was placed in our stairway tower. We didn't need a ladder to decorate—we just hung tinsel, ornaments, and lights as we went up the stairs. Daddy listed our gifts on the proverbial yellow pad so we could write our thank you notes.

One summer evening the sound of a guitar and singing wafted up to my room. I crept down the stairs to hear more. Daddy had invited Tito Guizar, a Mexican musician to entertain his guests. Tito later became a well-known Hollywood star, making dozens of films. Jim and I were thrilled to hear him perform at Winter Park's Langford Hotel in the '60's. He immediately remembered Daddy and told us that he had given him his start.

Day-to-day life was filled with fond memories. In the library, I sat on Daddy's lap as he taught me how to work crossword puzzles. As a grown woman, I still work a puzzle every day, and often come across words he taught me. They are a reminder of the precious times my father gave me.

Ed Thorgerson and his wife Nicki were often at our home. He was the voice for Fox Movietone News— Newsreels shown in movie theaters for many years. I loved his deep baritone voice.

The living room was off the front foyer and through double doors. Mommy would hang the "do not disturb" sign on the doors before a party...meaning forbidden territory to the boys. She prepared everything ahead of time, and as an adult, so do I.

She had tastefully filled the room with French furniture and a sofa in cut velvet. Her favorite ballet pictures that reminded her of those by Degas hung on the wall. Chinese lion bookends held special volumes and my favorite piece was a petite fireside table with a pull up silk screen to protect the wax on ladies faces from melting! The tiny table was the first item Mommy bought for the house. These treasures still belong to our family. The polished wood floors were covered with an antique Aubusson rug. I loved pretending I could play Beethoven's *Moonlight Sonata* on the Baldwin grand player-piano. Tall leaded windows overlooked the pond with matching French doors opening onto the flagstone terrace.

Grandmother Vivy was a domineering newspaper woman from Minneapolis. In her take charge manner, she told Mommy what to do, what was wrong with her, the

children, and the house. She was severe in her appearance. . .
usually dressed in a mannish suit with pince-nez spectacles
on her nose. Her wrists were adorned with a collection of
American Indian silver bracelets.

During one visit, Vivy rearranged the entire living room.
Daddy took her to the train, and Mommy put the furniture
back in its original place. Vivy had forgotten something, so
they returned unexpectedly. My mother was mortified at
being caught!

Helen Baxter was Mommy's
closest friend. They had graduated
together from the University of
Minnesota. A bubbly woman, Helen
was a fine portrait artist who built
my confidence in my artistic ability.
She did a pastel of me when I was
eight, wearing my usual white blouse and blue sweater.
Mommy had her ideas of how proper little girls should
dress. She virtually bought the same items in quantity —
white blouses, navy or brown pleated skirts, sweaters, and
jackets. It was like a school uniform. Once I was grown, I
never wore navy or brown again!

My best friend Iris Stafford and I entered Kindergarten
at Riverdale Country Day School. We walked home from

school together and often had sleep-overs, talking until late at night. I never went to church or Sunday school because Daddy said Christianity was a crutch and we "rugged individualists" didn't need a crutch.

I watched Iris kneeling at bedtime to say the Lord's Prayer. I sensed it was something important so I asked her to write it down for me. Once home, I hid the prayer because I thought my parents would disapprove. The Holy Spirit was putting a desire in my heart for God that He would someday bring to pass.

# 4

# Toys and Travel

On a family vacation to Nantucket, I had the winning raffle ticket for a one-room dollhouse furnished with Tudor style furnishings including a gateleg table set with pewter dinnerware, hutch, brick fireplace, and floral curtains at a leaded window. I played with it continually until one Christmas I received a two-story dollhouse from F.A.O. Schwartz. Iris and my friend Mary Haley named the small flexible family of dolls after the Banks family in *Mary Poppins*.

Iris moved to Long Island and when she visited me, she brought her unique portable train case. When opened, it was a replica of a Pullman compartment complete with camel-colored blankets like those on a real train. It had an upper berth, a fold-out lower berth, closet, and table that folded down between the seats. To come to my house, she packed the case full of her dollhouse toys. The way I pack as an adult was learned by using every inch of space in that toy.

One summer when Bill was at camp, I stayed in his room. Instead of my dormers, I enjoyed the view from the leaded windows on three sides of the room. But my favorite thing was removing the drawers from his kneehole desk and turning it into an apartment building with my doll house furniture.

I liked dolls and "Dye-Dee" doll was a favorite. She drank from a bottle and then wet her diaper. Dye-Dee slept in canopy bed and had a steamer trunk full of clothes. Then came the Dionne quintuplet dolls, fashioned after the real-life baby girls born in 1934—the first known case of quintuplets who all survived past infancy.

I learned much from watching Mommy decorate. On my thirteenth birthday my parents surprised me with a newly decorated bedroom. The wooden beds bore carved swans. My desk was topped with a bookcase complete with brass mesh doors. Inside I placed my favorite books, including *The Little Princess*, a Royal Crown Derby tea set that Vivy brought from England, clay teapot, and an antique cup and saucer. Spreads and shams were covered with dainty flowers. Hand-painted mirrored valances were mounted over each dormer. A comfy chair and skirted dressing table completed the picture. I spent a lot of time in my room up high in the tree tops.

I thought our basement would make a good game room. But the bathroom needed modernizing, so I painted the fixtures black like the marble ones in my mother's bathroom. My parents were not pleased, but in spite of ruining the fixtures...they redirected my talent to paper not porcelain.

Fun was easy to come by in Riverdale. I spent my summers swimming, and catching tadpoles, frogs, and crawfish in the pond. Winter days were spent sledding down the hills. A heavy snowfall meant building an igloo! When the pond froze, we laced up our skates and glided along the smooth ice. As it thawed, it gave a loud echoing snap! This was the sign to quickly jump to another piece, to avoid falling into the icy water. The boys played ice hockey. One year Burr's head was cut by a skate. He was carried to our house with blood pouring from his wound. Mommy cried as she watched the doctor lay Burr on the dining room table to stitch up his head! She had a hard time with the ways of boys. Football, fighting, and roughhousing were not her cup of tea. When she heard too much noise upstairs, she would shout, "Whatever you're doing up there, stop it!"

I still had a great deal of freedom as a child…bike riding or roller skating for hours on the smooth private streets. I walked to a bus stop to go to the movies…followed up by a ham and cheese on rye, with a milkshake at the local soda shop.

One Sunday I was invited to Brucie Hughes' house for lunch. Her grandfather sat at the head of the table, all dressed in black, with a long white beard. He seemed quite formidable. As well he should have; he was the Chief Justice of the United States!

Everyone had finished eating when I noticed that I had some milk left in my glass. I quickly drank it down and just as quickly it came up….all over the Chief Justice! Later I learned that Brucies' grandfather, Charles Evans Hughes had been governor of New York and narrowly lost the race for the presidency against Woodrow Wilson!

One summer, we drove my brothers to Camp Yonanoka in Linville, North Carolina. On the way we stopped in Williamsburg, Virginia. The Governor's Palace had just opened. In the Grand Ballroom, the tour guide asked if anyone could locate the one bird on the exquisite Chinese wallpaper. I was excited to find it! In Linville, we stayed at Chetola Lodge. More than forty years later, driving through Linville, I said, "Oh, I stayed there when I was seven!" Jim responded, "You couldn't possibly remember that." "When you are a New Yorker and you stay in a place covered with Chestnut bark, you remember it!"

When I was eight, I went to Ecole Champlain, a French-speaking camp in Vermont. My father had learned French when he was stationed in France during WWI, and frequently spoke French to us at the dinner table. I enjoyed the camp craft work most, and the horseback riding the least. My assigned horse was Belle. She was old, slow, and—from my perspective—as tall as a skyscraper. Riding round and round in the ring was boring, but Greg the groomsman was tall, dark, and handsome! My type at that age!

Our family took winter vacations in Sarasota, Florida. My mother and I rode the train, armed with books to read. I chuckle as I recall Violet, a precocious little girl trying to cope with her divorced parents. . . written in the '30s when divorce was scandalous. I spent time looking out our compartment window and listening to the "ding-ding-ding" at the crossings. As we rode through the south, I saw rundown shacks and barely clothed children—a new sight that saddened me. How different was my way of life.

**Iris, Mommy, and Nina**

In Sarasota, we stayed on the Gulf at the Mira Mar Hotel. It was surrounded by quaint gift shops where I found glass animals to add to my collection. In the mornings on our way to the beach, we stopped at a stand for fresh squeezed orange juice. On leaving, the lady would say, "Ya'll hur' back." So we named the stand "Hurback's."

I was quite young when we took a coastal cruise up the eastern seaboard to Maine. Daddy gave me a teddy bear to keep me company. "What will you name him?" he asked. I had noticed a tag on his neck that read "Washable." I assumed that was his name. I treasured "Washable" for years until he came to a fateful end.

His loss was as bad as the day my canary, Billie, met his fate. Billie's home was a brass cage on a stand in the dining room, where he sang the day away. Because moths had eaten the red wool yarn in our oriental rug, the fumigator had to be called. Poor Billie was forgotten and met the same end as the color-conscious moths. I cried when Daddy put Billie in his grave.

"Washable," on the other hand, was cremated. I don't remember much about being quarantined with Scarlet Fever but my pajamas, linens, toys, all had to be burned. "Washable" joined the pyre.

Because I missed too much school to be promoted, I would have to repeat the fourth grade. My parents, fearing my embarrassment, decided to send me away to school. Being separated from home, family, and friends was a painful time. Did mixed messages ever enter my young mind? *You chose me yet now you are sending me away. Did I do something wrong? Is it my fault?*

The plane dipped beneath the clouds, and a sudden drop interrupted my daydream. Dropping a little at 30,000 feet didn't frighten me anymore. I wasn't that scared little girl. By then, I knew my life was designed by God; His love had expelled my fear. Everything that happened was part of His plan, including going to boarding school at age nine. I am sure my parents thought it was the best option—but it couldn't have been an easy decision for them, particularly my mother. Even today, I remember that knot inside of me.

# 5

# Scarborough

Forty-five minutes north of my home was the unfamiliar, friendless building where I lived Monday through Friday. As a grown woman returning to visit, that knot pulled tight again when I came over one particular hill near school...it meant "we were almost there." I recall how Mommy and I hardly spoke a word every Sunday afternoon. It was tortuous for us both.

I stayed at Scarborough through the eighth grade, going home only for weekends, holidays, and summers. I exchanged my tree top room for an impersonal dorm room, with new faces for parents and friends.

I had a single room as there weren't any boarders my age. My two teenage suite-mates mothered and nurtured me. They braided my hair, helped me select outfits, and took me to classes. Bless them!

Summers had changed; my friends now had their own best friends. I was the outsider. When I wasn't traveling or busy with family, I was content in my tree top room reading, drawing, and listening to the radio. I would daydream about a sister...wondering if there was someone out there like me? My parents never hid the knowledge that I had a younger sister.

Summertime meant eating meals on the terrace. At a ladies luncheon, a stray dog appeared on the terrace after his dip in the pond. He was so eager for affection that he jumped up, putting dirty paw patterns on the ladies' white dresses! Mommy had never favored dogs. At age five, I had my one and only dog, a Scottie named Mickey. That day on the terrace was when I ended up with a canary!

In my third year at Scarborough, my new roommate was Gina Glanton. It was the start of a very close friendship that lasted all our adult lives. She was like the sister I dreamed about.

The Christmas Pageant at Scarborough involved the entire student body and made a lasting impact on me. The Nativity Scene was center stage in our spacious auditorium. The Three Magi wore majestic costumes as they walked down the two aisles. We younger students followed as part of their entourage. The organ played "Oh Holy Night." As the words were sung, "Fall on your knees, oh hear the angel voices" we all bowed face down to the floor. I didn't understand the meaning, but it stirred something in my heart. Through all these years, when that hymn is sung, I picture myself lying prostrate before Him.

During summer vacations, Gina spent weeks with me in Riverdale. Her home life was not easy, so she loved being part of our family. We would turn on the record player and sing from memory most of the scores of *Carousel* or *Oklahoma*. Mommy took us to numerous Broadway shows, but those were our two favorites.

Our mothers became good friends. Virginia was younger, glamorous, and a stylish dresser. Mommy was more conservative, but Virginia began to influence her, starting with her hat selections. I remember a perky black one with a flower sticking straight up and a polka dot veil. I could tell it made Mommy feel special.

The two often lunched together in the city. But when Mommy came home, she was different...strange. She had been drinking. There was a sadness in her eyes and I could hear her crying quietly in her room. Why was she unhappy? As I got older, it became more acute, and often embarrassed me. Sometimes when I tried to talk to her she didn't make sense and became morose. Like many, she drank in an attempt to drown out her unhappy married life. Both she and Daddy had a private life apart from the family. They had stayed together because of the commitment they made earlier regarding their children, perhaps for propriety, and because of the difficulty of divorce in those days. My brothers and I never spoke of Mommy's attempt to cope, but it affected me deeply. I still despise alcohol because it controls, twists, and destroys the people I love.

Scarborough was no longer lonely because of Gina. In the seventh grade we moved into a new dorm, a stately old brick building that had been a private residence.

As budding decorators, we loved continually rearranging our furniture. A downstairs kitchen was available, and a solarium for games and dancing. We were introduced to sewing by making broomstick skirts—a skirt-length piece of fabric was sewn to a waistband, dampened, and wound around a broomstick until it dried. Voila! A skirt with crinkled pleats!

On school free days, Gina and I would take the train to the city to shop, eat hot fudge sundaes at Schrafft's, and go to the big movie theaters in Times Square or Radio City. Sometimes Mommy met us and took us to the Plaza for lunch or tea in the Palm Court. Gina and I were so excited when we purchased our first silk stockings. If one stocking had a run, we would use Rit Dye to make it match another. They were hard to come by as silk was being used for parachutes in the war.

While shopping with Mommy, she introduced me to several salesladies who had become her friends. "Woody," a statuesque white-haired lady at Bergdorf's, was one of her favorites. When I married, Woody covered an old coin with satin to place in my shoe on my wedding day.

Mommy loved helping people...giving gifts, her time, a listening ear, and money. It was her nature to give and perhaps she also recalled those days when she had come from Canada and struggled to make ends meet.

Subtle changes came about as I adapted to life at Scarborough; there were shortages of once common items, a new seriousness on people's faces, and troubling news from faraway places. I began making more friends, and even had my first kiss. But life was on the brink of change for me, for my family, and the whole world.

# 6

# Learning to Pray

I stretched my legs as best I could in the restrictive cabin of the plane. The hum of the engine had lulled some to sleep. The stewardess returned, and I took the juice she offered. My hand trembled as I held the cup. The excitement of meeting Barbara increased as the plane got closer to New York.

As a student at Scarborough, a new fear entered my life—War! Before December 1941, I hadn't paid much attention to adult talk about events overseas. But our family listened regularly to FDR's radio "Fireside Chats." Mommy hung on every word, knowing her sons might enlist. Daddy was definitely not a fan of President Roosevelt. On Sunday afternoon of December 7th, as Mommy and I listened to the opera from the Met, a voice interrupted the broadcast to announce that the Japanese had attacked Pearl Harbor and many lives were lost.

Talk of war escalated. In my child's imagination, I visualized bombs dropping on all of us. Men were going off to war, and women were taking jobs normally filled by men. We now had ration cards and stamps for gas, meat, butter, sugar, even tires.

Live-in servants were no longer with us. For the first time in her married life, Mommy was cooking! Her menu was limited, but I enjoyed the delicious buttered flounder and salads with homemade dressing of oil and vinegar seasoned with fresh herbs. Desserts were a thing of the past.

From a broadcasted Fireside chat:

*It is the task of our generation, yours and mine to build and defend not for our generation alone. We defend the foundations laid down by our fathers. We build a life for generations yet unborn. We defend and we build a way of life, not for America alone, but for all mankind. Ours is a high duty, a noble task.*

*Day and night I pray for the restoration of peace in this mad world of ours. It is not necessary that I, the President ask the American people to pray in behalf of such a cause— for I know you are praying with me.*

*I am certain that out of the hearts of every man, woman and child in this land, in every waking minute, a supplication goes up to Almighty God; that all of us beg that suffering and starving, that death and destruction may end — and that peace may return to the world. In common affection for all mankind, your prayers join with mine — that God will heal the wounds and the hearts of humanity.*

When the sirens blew, we were subject to a blackout drill. Black curtains now hung on all our windows. Inspectors came knocking if even a sliver of light could be seen from our house.

My parents did their part to aid the war effort. Mommy worked with Bundles for Britain, a project started by a knitting group that met in a Manhattan storefront. Ladies knitted sweaters, scarves, and caps that were shipped to soldiers in England. Bundles also sent clothing, rolled bandages, and medical supplies for the men in the field.

Daddy's patriotism led him to be involved in numerous engineering projects such as dry-docks in Alabama for the building of ships and oil tankers. He received several honorary medals for his work during the war.

My brother Bill was seriously dating Mary Fickett, daughter of Homer Fickett, director of the radio drama, "Theater Guild of the Air." Our

**Bill (c) and war buddies**

families were good friends (Mary went on to star in "All My Children" for twenty years). Bill couldn't wait to fight the enemy so he enlisted! Through Daddy's friendship with Admiral Ben Morell, Bill joined the Navy Seabees. Bill the risk taker was a deep-sea diver, repairing underwater ship and dock damage. He participated in the D-Day invasion in France and then was sent to the Pacific Theater; stationed in Iwo Jima. He sent Mommy everything from a Japanese flag to a bayonet. That only added to her anxiety about her son in danger. To "keep up the morale," I wrote weekly letters to my brothers.

Burr, tall like Daddy and very handsome, had started at Columbia University, his father's alma mater. He sang tenor with the Columbia Chorus, even performing at Carnegie Hall. I attended as a youngster. What were "Dem Dry Bones" all about? *La Boheme* was his favorite opera and he often went about the house singing parts of the score. It too, became my favorite and was the first opera I went to at the Metropolitan.

**Burr**

Having my brothers in the war was frightening. Especially for Burr, as his temperament was contemplative, sensitive, and creative. He fulfilled his duty by enlisting in the Army, but health issues kept him stateside.

Daily living in the Spencer household was simpler, yet simplicity didn't cover the uncertainty of world events or the possibility of danger coming to our shores. Stories were circulating about submarines off our East Coast.

My imagination ran away as I watched the Blitz in London on the Newsreels. Could that happen in Riverdale? That is when I said my first prayer. Did Mommy put aside her sadness and pray for her sons? Did Daddy, despite his unbelief, pray? Yet one little girl in the top of that house tried to speak to God. I didn't know Who He was, but He knew me and He was pursuing me.

*"I have called you by name, you are mine"* (Isaiah 43:1).

We never knew what became of our German servants. We heard about the Japanese camps, but little about the German-Americans who were interred. One such camp was at Ellis Island, where possibly Mia and Mary Peanut went. The place that had once welcomed immigrants now became the place that held them captive, or sent them back to their homeland.

While the war was continuing, my parents selected a new school for me. I never knew the reason. It offered more opportunities and a fine art department. Once there, I went home only for summers and holidays.

# 7

# Penn Hall

In 1944, I entered Penn Hall, a girl's school in Chambersburg, Pennsylvania. Gina and her family had moved to California. This was another opportunity to adjust. The school was larger, more academic, but it was the place I would spend the next four years. Still shy initially, I began to venture out. Separation was teaching me independence. In the forties, independence and self-reliance were the name of the game.

From New York I took the train and a bus to Chambersburg. The town seemed old-fashioned and backward to me. The campus was still impressive with its red brick buildings supported by stately white columns. In the background rose soft blue-grey mountains. Each floor of the dormitories had suites of two bedrooms joined by a bath. I had a roommate and two suite mates. School life was full of studies and activities, which made for an easier adjustment. I loved the esprit de corps and many life-long friendships were made there. It was an exceptional school and that was demonstrated by the fact that long after it closed, the alumnae remained active. Publications were continually sent and reunions were held. Many have said they spent their happiest years at Penn Hall. I have been class correspondent since 1948.

I was involved in student government, class projects, and ardently stayed out of all athletic programs. The fully equipped Art Department was a world in which to learn my craft. Other favorite subjects were music appreciation, art studio, history, writing, and English literature. Being familiar with French, it was my choice for a language credit; but my counselor was the Latin teacher, so I took Latin. With a bad attitude, I failed her course. The following years, I returned to French.

Chapel was a daily requirement, where for the first time I heard the old traditional hymns. I listened with curiosity and awe. I didn't understand their meaning, but they took root in me. I still can hear the words of many:

*What a Friend we have in Jesus,*
*all our sins and grief's to bear!*
*What a privilege to carry*
*everything to God in prayer!*
*O what peace we often forfeit,*
*O what needless pain we bear.*
*All because we do not carry*
*everything to God in prayer.*

Was this the same Jesus who hung on the little palm cross in the room of Mia and Mary Peanut? How could He be my friend? Didn't He die long ago?

I took comfort from the words of hymns during that time of uncertainty.

*O God, our help in ages past, our hope for years to come,*
*Our shelter from the stormy blast, and our eternal home.*

In wartime, we needed a shelter from the stormy blast. On Sundays, church attendance was required. My roommate and I had never been to church, so we chose the one with the handsome boys in the choir. I paid little attention to the sermons, so they had no effect on my daily living.

Mercersburg, a nearby boys' school, came for Saturday dates and occasional dances. In my second year at school, the war ended. Soldiers came home and life returned to a new kind of normal.

Sacrificial and hard times were over and our country experienced an economic boom. Some women remained in the work force. New houses went up, new jobs were created. The nightmares of the past years were seemingly over, but certainly not forgotten.

Burr visited me at school a few times and my classmates were all giggles at having a handsome man on campus. He gradually became my confidant, helping with my school decisions and giving me advice about friendships.

In my junior year, Burr returned to break the news that Mommy and Daddy were divorcing. I was shocked! Burr helped me understand that their search for a temporary marital resolution and vow to raise a family had been accomplished. The struggle was over. Mommy would go to Reno for six weeks to get the divorce. But there was more...Daddy was going to marry Irene, who had been part of his life for some time. I wondered who Irene was.

Mommy left Riverdale and moved into a suite at the Carlyle Hotel until our penthouse on 71st and Fifth Avenue was completed. I took living at the Carlyle for granted, I had no idea it was a very prestigious hotel. We admired their famous Bemelmans murals, ate in the elegantly appointed dining room or had Agnes, our maid prepare our meals upstairs.

In my senior year I decided to enroll at Parsons. Miss Gertrude Meyer, my art teacher, meaning to prepare me told me that after completing a project at Parsons, the instructor might tear it up right in front of me. Timid Nina immediately changed her plans! I missed many opportunities because of my fears. Forgoing an education at Parsons was one of them.

In my last two years at school, classmates and I took weekend trips to West Point. I had been to a college weekend once but I didn't like the partying and drinking. West Point had athletic events, parades, football games, and dances – good clean fun. Sometimes I had a blind date, and other times I dated a particular cadet. Attending Army-Navy games in Philadelphia was now more fun.

Graduation day arrived. Tears were shed as we said our goodbyes. The baccalaureate service gave me a lot to ponder. *What kind of life would I live? What was in my future?* I left many dear friends and returned to my new home in Manhattan.

Daddy was still a big part of my life. We often lunched together at the Columbia Club. Gradually I became more comfortable visiting him and Irene in Riverdale. His new wife was someone I would grow to love.

The next fall I entered Barmore College in Manhattan to study art, design, writing, radio, and advertising. I was also training at the Conover Modeling Agency with the promise of a job. At the end of our training we were each to make a brief speech. I was paralyzed with fear! The teacher graciously asked me to step down. Public speaking more than frightened me!

Conover found a modeling job for me with Claire McCardell in the Garment District on Sixth Avenue. She was my favorite designer and I already owned some of her clothes. Claire, a graduate of Parsons, was considered one of the best new designers in the industry. She was a real trendsetter. . . designing pleated pants for women, and reintroducing the Empire look with spaghetti straps winding around the bodice. Claire used exquisite fabrics—tweeds, linen, silks, and wool. In recent years, some of her collection has been on display at the Metropolitan Museum. Working for her allowed me to purchase many samples. Then I was selected to sell and take orders from the buyers. I felt uncomfortable doing that, so I resigned and left with my McCardell purchases.

There was a certain handsome young man who also found that style attractive.

# 8

# Some Enchanted Evening

My life in the city seemed glamorous. I lived in a penthouse overlooking Central Park, worked for my favorite designer, and enjoyed the activities of a large city. Joan Bulkley, my former suite-mate, invited me to a "Sadie Hawkins" dance in Darien, Connecticut. It was August 7, 1948. I wore a soft yellow formal dress with the required elbow-length white leather gloves.

I glanced across the crowded room and saw a tall, dark, handsome young man in a white dinner jacket. Our eyes met and my heart began to race at the sight of him. I was too shy to even imagine a conversation with him. Joan introduced us—his name was Jim Locke: self-assured, charismatic, and with an obvious gift of gab. He frightened this shy wallflower.

At a "Sadie Hawkins" dance, the girls take the lead — driving, buying a boutonniere, and asking the men to dance. I asked everyone at our table except Jim. That piqued his curiosity — or perhaps his pride. The last dance was a number dance. Jim found the man who held my number and exchanged tickets. Despite my trembling as we danced and that I hardly spoke, he asked to see me again. In a few days I was leaving for California to see Gina. *Would I ever hear from him again?*

A train ride alone across the country was an adventure for a seventeen year old. Gina's family didn't have a guest room, so Mommy arranged for me to spend a month at the Beverly Wilshire Hotel. Gina and I swam in the pool, sunbathed, ate in the dining room or ordered room service. We visited movie sets, had lunch at the Brown Derby, and saw a sneak preview of "Kiss of Death" with Victor Mature and introducing Richard Widmark. The time with Gina renewed our friendship, eased the hurt of my parent's divorce as well as my concerns about my future.

At Barmore College I made friends with Nancy Day from Hastings. In December I would make my debut at the Waldorf. The evening before, Mommy gave me a lovely party in the Victorian Suite at the Carlyle. I invited Jim, but he didn't respond or come.

Our Waldorf table was filled with family and guests. Gina and Nancy were there. My escort was West Point cadet, Dick Gillespie. He arranged a blind date for Nancy with Roy Henderson; they later married. After dinner, the debs with their escorts walked in a line around the room being introduced by name. The cadets in their handsome uniforms made the evening even more festive.

Jim was not there, yet he was not out of my thoughts.

One day while taking a Fifth Avenue bus to work, I saw Jim! I stepped off the bus and began casually walking towards IBM where he worked. My plan was that as I passed him, he would see me, tap me on the shoulder, and say, "Fancy seeing *you* here." There was no tap. Jim was gone. Turning back, I glanced into a coffee shop, and he was there! Wearing a black dress with a red and white polka dot beret and scarf, I strolled in and said, "Jim Locke, fancy seeing *you* here." He asked me to join him for a cup of coffee. I had never had coffee before; and I found myself saying I enjoyed it even though I really didn't. That was my first and only cup of coffee in my whole life. But it wasn't the last I would see of Jim Locke.

A year had passed since the night we danced. Three days after our "accidental" encounter, Jim called and asked me if I would join him for an evening with his friend Gene Page in Levittown, Long Island. Driving there, as far as we could see were acres of little cookie cutter houses covering the treeless landscape. The houses were so similar that on occasion, returning from work, a man would enter the wrong house. The subdivision was built for servicemen who qualified for the GI Bill. We played Parcheesi that night and I noticed that Jim was quite competitive.

Four days later we went to the Hayden Planetarium to see a spectacular presentation of stars and planets. We giggled at the unexpected sight of a couple of little white mice scurrying across the floor. After the show, we went to the Polo bar at the Westbury Hotel near my home. In spite of my usual shyness, talking with Jim was easy. We chatted for a long time, discovering that we had a mutual love of antiques, old houses, and many other things. That night, I knew I was falling in love with dashing Jim.

Just three days later—on July 31, 1949—he proposed, and I said yes.

He was twenty-three, and I was nineteen. We were young, naïve, and *so* in love. It brought to mind the words from a "Hello Dolly" song…"It only took a moment…to be loved a whole life long."

Jim, a gentleman to the core, went to my father and asked his permission to marry me. Daddy, wise though loving, asked us to wait a year. Without hesitation, Jim said, "Of course, sir."

Jim and I picked out a ring and on October 30th we announced our engagement. Then Mommy and I began to plan our wedding. Since we were not a church-going family, we looked in the Yellow Pages for a church. When we visited Central Presbyterian Church on Park Avenue, we felt it was the right one. It was traditional and the Park Avenue address was impressive and would look good on an invitation. Dr. Theodore Speers, the minister, gave us brief but godly counsel before our wedding.

We never forgot his admonition:

*"What therefore GOD hath joined together, let not man put asunder"* (Mark 10:9).

Dr. Speers had been an honored shot-put athlete at Princeton, and later served as the West Point Chaplain. We joined the church and in coming years he christened our three children. He shared the Gospel with us, but we weren't ready to respond. He was another one placed in my path that ultimately brought me to God. By providence we had

chosen the right minister to marry us. It was not just the address!

Clouds suddenly enveloped the plane, and I went back to thoughts of our wedding. My mother, in spite of her reservations about our being so young, and making a decision after three dates, was enthusiastic and supportive. My happiness meant everything to her. Her first decision was to reserve The Terrace Room at the Plaza for our reception.

I designed my satin gown with antique lace at the neck, leg o'mutton sleeves, and a hoop skirt with old-fashioned padded hips. My inspiration was drawn from movie stars like Greer Garson who appeared in my favorite romantic period films.

May 6, 1950. Mommy had arranged a garden setting in the church: spring flowers and live dogwood trees. She wore a deep purple silk dress. Jim's mother wore soft green. Dear Rose helped me dress. I slipped Woody's satin-covered coin into my shoe as "something old."

There were six bridesmaids: Iris, three Penn Hall friends, Jim's sister Janie, and Nancy from college. Gina was my Maid of Honor. Susan, Burr's wife, was the Matron of Honor. They all wore yellow organdy dresses and carried deep purple tulips with lavender lilacs. Jim's father was his best man.

Lester Lanin's popular orchestra played at the reception. Gina caught the bouquet (as planned). She was dating Jim's

IBM friend, Bryce Ainsley. After the reception, we took a carriage ride through Central Park. Our wedding night was spent at the Biltmore Hotel, a favorite spot of ours. We had often met "under the clock." It was known as a convenient rendezvous place for young people.

We honeymooned at the Cloisters in Sea Island, Georgia. Beauty, elegance and service surrounded us like a fairytale. Jim's mother's friend Kit and her husband Bill Jones owned the Cloisters. At the honeymoon breakfast in front of thirty couples, I introduced myself as Nina Spencer. *Oops.*

Our first home was an apartment in Peter Cooper Village, a well-known post WWII housing development on the East River in lower Manhattan. They had a long waiting list, but Daddy arranged for us to have an apartment on the tenth floor at 1090 First Avenue. The rooms were exceptionally large and our monthly rent was $110! We chose Country French antiques and Mommy helped us select fabrics for the upholstered pieces.

Dogs were not allowed, so my poodle "Lambsie" remained with my mother. After Gina and Bryce married, Daddy helped them locate in a nearby apartment. Other young married friends chose Peter Cooper including my suite-mate Joan and her husband Bert deSelding. Jim and I became fast friends with Virginians Jack and Susan Hagan, who lived down the hall.

I liked being a wife and enjoyed keeping a nice home, but I knew little about cooking. Jim told me that one of the wives we had met at The Cloisters, made her husband pancakes every day for breakfast. Not to be outdone, I looked for a pancake recipe in my cookbook collection. Literally an hour later, with flour all over me and a kitchen filled with dirty dishes, I brought forth the pancakes...do I hear a drum roll, please!

"Nancy Port may do this every morning," I said. "But I'm not."

Quietly, Jim asked, "Have you ever heard of Aunt Jemima?"

"No, who is she?" I had spent the morning making fancy French crepes!

Shortly after our marriage, Mommy told us about my grandmother Chasey. They had stayed in touch since my adoption and my mother thought it was time for me to know about my birth family. I was fascinated to learn that Chasey was a portrait artist who had lived in England and Paris and socialized with famous painters, sculptors, and musicians.

She lived in Albany now and if Mommy had no objection, I wanted to meet her. I knew little about Ethel Chase, but she knew a lot about me...mostly about my beginnings. She had a story to tell and I wanted to listen.

# 9

# Chasey

*Chase's Mills, via Buckfield, Maine*
*September 20, 1931*

*My Dear Mrs. Spencer,*

*For some reason, perhaps the to-be-expected reaction to what led up to my leaving Denia with you, though I have started several letters to you, I have been completely unable to finish them, even though I knew Mr. Spencer would be expecting my promised letter... I am not in this letter going to attempt to really say anything, except this, to perhaps ease your own mind a bit, i.e. I am completely at ease in my mind as to Denia's well-being and happiness; my suffering is for myself and NOT for her. My Cousin Helen's messages of your joy in her have convinced me of what I already knew. Denia's mother has accepted the conditions as they are, so that is all right.*

*There are times in life when one must simply hold oneself taut in a period of endurance until the passing weeks or months shall give one more strength. You are the guardian of one who is the most precious human being in my life... I cannot say more... I*

*love her so much that I can only feel love for those who love her,
and so I sign myself.*

*With Affection,*
*E. Chase-MacColl*

In the early 1930s, my grandmother, Ethel Chase MacColl, found herself caring for the child of her daughter, Moragh. Some women in those circumstances would take on the role of parent and raise another generation. Chasey, an artist trying to support herself during the Great Depression, was unable to take the path expected of her. Hearing how she loved me and didn't give me up easily brought me some resolution.

With Jim's support, a meeting was arranged. When I saw my diminutive, white-haired, natural grandmother, her expression was one of love, fulfillment and gratitude. She believed she would never see me again.

She wanted to know about my life, I wanted to know about hers. Full of energy, enthusiasm, there was excitement in her voice and even in the way she moved. The glint in her eyes faded momentarily as she said, "I haven't heard of my daughter in years." I learned some things about my birth mother that day.

Moragh had refused to divulge my father's identity to anyone, including her own mother. Some of the information

Chasey had written to Daddy turned out to be pure fiction. My birth certificate, for the sake of decency, bore the last name Disturl, invented by Chasey.

Moragh demonstrated no maternal tendencies so Chasey had full care of a baby. After a time she had to make the painful decision to give her only granddaughter up for adoption. She wrote the following letter to my father:

*Chase's Mills, via Buckfield, Maine*
*September 20, 1931*

*My Dear Mr. Spencer,*

*I have attempted to explain in a letter to Mrs. Spencer the reasons for the delay in writing my promised particulars as to Denia's parentage.*

*Denia, as you will doubtless have guessed, is illegitimate. Her father was of Welsh descent; a gentleman by birth and education. Denia's mother, on her father's side, is the granddaughter of a Highland Scottish gentleman who spent an active life in the Far East where he married a daughter of the then Governor of Java, who later became Prime Minister of Holland. Through myself, Denia is the eleventh generation in America; the lineal descendant of Benjamin West, second President of the Royal Academy in England, and of Hannibal Hamlin, Vice-President with Lincoln, and is the great-granddaughter of Solon Chase, founder of the Greenback Party and its nominee for the Presidency.*

*With kindest regards,*
*Very sincerely,*
*E. Chase-MacColl*

She gave the Spencer's some information about me that in her mind was redeeming of her daughter's behavior. I had come from good stock, though my mother was a woman without moral character. The mention of Hannibal Hamlin and Solon Chase were based on fact. The other descendants may have been more of Chasey's stories—she didn't lack in creativity. Her Mother, Drusilla Hamlin, was a direct descendant of Hannibal Hamlin—Vice President under Lincoln. He was a State Senator in Maine and later the Ambassador to Spain.

**Drusilla by Chasey**

Chasey's eyes, words, and her body language convinced me that giving me away had been devastating. She had nurtured me for almost two years! There was grief and disappointment in her daughter and then the forever loss of Denia.

Chasey fascinated me. My upbringing and temperament made me reserved, refined in manners, and behavior. Here was a woman who showed excitement without restraint. She lived life with an artist's soul. Born and raised in Maine, she attended the Art Institute in New York when she was in her teens. A free spirit–perhaps one of the first hippies—she had backpacked across Europe in the early 1900s, gaining a dubious reputation because she had "bobbed" her hair and smoked cigarettes.

Somewhere along her travels, she met and married William Dugald MacColl, a Scottish historian from Fort William. They had one daughter. Her full name was Hermine Elizabeth Frances Nevadita Emily George Piqui Hadi-Bada Moragh Chase-MacColl. Moragh is Scottish, Hermine was a cousin, and Nevadita was a spiritualist writer in India. Chasey called Moragh, Piqui.

Marriage for the tempestuous Chasey did not last. She left her husband, and for a while her daughter was in his care. Eventually fearing his influence over her, Chasey executed a late-night kidnapping of Moragh. She claimed the ordeal turned her hair white overnight! Two of the following generations prove that early white hair is genetic in our family.

Chasey continued her bohemian lifestyle, painting ivory miniatures at the Tate Gallery in London, living on the Isle of Man, and listening to Rachmaninoff play as Moragh danced. Imagine! That first day, Chasey gave me her tiny black metal paint box. It was held in the palm of her hand with a ring that slipped over her pinky. As she painted on ivory, she would mix colors from the small cubes of paint onto the fold-out palette. Everything she needed was nestled inside this rare little box, which today is mine.

She spent years in Paris studying and socializing with artists and writers. Her art was realistic and Impressionism was on the rise. Politics were shifting and science was going beyond the bounds of accepted beliefs. No longer bound by truth of color and nature, the newer artist's work came from their imagination. Perhaps this was a reason why Chasey returned to America.

She knew authors like Hemingway, playwright George Bernard Shaw, and was a close friend of Sculptor Jo Davidson, who mentions her in his autobiography, Between Sittings. Chasey also admired expatriate poet Ezra Pound, who was part of the Modernist Movement. He was later arrested for treason during WW II. Voices of liberalism and socialism were demanding to be heard. Views of Nietzsche, Darwin, Marx, Einstein, and Freud were becoming popular and acceptable.

This environment was where Chasey raised her little girl...surrounded by great talent but without a stable home life and never attending the same school for more than a year. Chasey moved like the wind and before Moragh was grown, the two moved back to New York. Numerous clients wanted her kind of portraiture. She became engrossed in painting portraits of high society, stage, civic leaders, and physicians. She gave me a large oil portrait of the wife of poet Oreck Johns — the only original piece of work I own.

**Grace Johns by Chasey**

For Fifty years, Grace Lambert, a patron of the arts, was the financial supporter for Chasey's diverse endeavors. In 1960, Chasey appeared on Grace's doorstep...saying she wanted to live her senior days in Princeton. Grace found two rooms to rent in the home of the Boconfussios'. They took care of her needs and loved her.

On May 19, 1920, Moragh's tenth birthday, Chasey began *A Book of Bees*. Each page was a reminder to the reader of a virtue. Be truthful, be courageous, be honest, and so on.

*May she be as busy as a bee, going out each day into the*
*sunshine of helpfulness, wisdom, and loyalty to fill the*
*bowl of her life with the honey of sweet thoughts gathered*
*from the flowers of faith, love and remembrance.*
*From her Buddie Chasey*

The first page of this little green book says, "In memory of the bees that came to live and work at Peartree Farm in Yorkshire, England." Chasey had drawn a little beehive above the table of contents.

One chapter was called "Concerning What Hadi-Bada Learns of Other Bees." This was where her daughter was to write a response. The Bees were to encourage Moragh to be good, loyal, wise, truthful, helpful, gentle, thoughtful, reverent, and busy. Tragically for Chasey, these were qualities that her daughter lacked throughout her life. In 1925, in Westport Connecticut, Moragh had written her response to "Be thoughtful": *I try to be thoughtful but it is very hard sometimes. I try to think of this little book and all that was written in it by the sweetest mother in the world who has always tried to teach me to do what is right.*

In 1929 Chasey began a similar green book for Denia. I have both copies.

*Chase's Mills, via Buckfield, Maine*
*October 8, 1931*

*Dear Mr. Spencer,*

*I am so grateful for your letter…it makes my feeling of ease as regards Denia, complete. Thank you…My plans, as regards returning to New York, are very uncertain – I will let you know as soon as they are definite… At present I am busily taking a "cure" painting the amazingly beautiful out-of-doors which Maine so feverously offers – and consequently, am feeling a thousand times better!*

*Denia's birthday is November 13th. I can't remember if I told you that the quaint little gold chain which she wore was a part of my father's engagement present to my mother.*

*With much affection,*
*E. Chase MacColl*

After taking me to Riverdale, Chasey retreated to the land in Maine, at Teague's Hill to draw from her roots and recover from her losses.

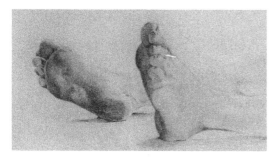

**Drawing by Chasey**

She returned to the city and was hired by the New York City Morgue as part of the W.P.A. government works program for the unemployed during the Depression. It was an instrument to find work for artists, writers and millions of others.

Chasey was hired to depict the condition of the deceased, dismembered bodies, murder and accident victims, and record the evidence. Not a desirable job, but it was a living. The Medical Examiner's Deputies tried to make her pass out, throw up, or quit. But remaining strong, Chasey later was honored in a ceremony at which Dr. Milton

Helpern, Chief Medical Examiner (CME) presented her with her own key to the morgue!

From there she worked in the Psychiatric Department of Mount Sinai Hospital, drawing conté crayon sketches of hands of the mentally ill. Doctors used them to help diagnose and treat patients.

She told me about drawing the hands of a catatonic patient. The next day he pried open his window and jumped to his death. The attending psychiatrist viewed Chasey's drawings and said, "If I had seen the drawing sooner, I might have treated him differently and perhaps saved him."

While there, she began teaching weaving as therapy for the patients. This led to the formation of her own business *Gadred Weavers*. She had a sixteen-harness loom made, which she donated to the Cooper-Hewitt Design Museum in New York.

Grace Lambert told me that Albert Einstein and Chasey played chess in Princeton. Imagine those two white heads competing — the artist and the genius!

For years Chasey wrote what she called "Scribblings," filling numerous volumes of black three-ring notebooks. This ended when she broke her hip and went into a nursing home. In 1967, the pages of her life were closed in Princeton. Volumes of "Scribbling's" were never found.

# 10

# Moragh

Flying to meet my sister, I wondered what she knew of Chasey and our birth mother. In the 1950 meeting with my grandmother, I learned that I also had two half-brothers in England. Chasey had been close to Peter, so she left all her belongings to him. However when she died, nothing was sent to him. A lot of our family history was lost.

While I was in Chasey's care, Moragh became pregnant with Barbara. This time the father's identity was not a secret. His mother insisted they marry and she would provide an apartment and everything they needed. However, when she discovered that her new daughter-in-law already had a baby by another man, she ended the support and the relationship.

Chasey, having undergone the heartbreak of losing her first grandchild, bowed out as caregiver for the new baby. With her Manhattan connections she found a temporary home with the Gertrude Vanderbilt Whitney family. They named the baby Barbara after the youngest Whitney daughter. Adopted at fourteen months, neither mother nor grandmother ever had any contact with Barbara.

A darkness had taken root in Moragh. She was a troubled young woman who seemed to be searching for the love of a man. She was beautiful, tall and thin with long delicate fingers, dark hair, and big brown eyes. Those eyes showed no joy, only want.

She connected with her father, who brought her back to England. He then encouraged her to marry an older gentleman. He thought this would end her

**Peter and Michael**

reckless ways. It did not. Moragh and Jack Goldsmith had two boys, Peter and Michael. The boys' story, not surprisingly, was one of pain and loss.

The bombings in London were increasing. Children who had relatives in America were allowed to enter the States — reminiscent of the children in *Tales of Narnia* who were sent to the English countryside. Moragh and her young boys boarded one of the last ships leaving England and sailed for New York. They lived in New Jersey with Chasey until she told her daughter she couldn't keep the boys indefinitely. One day, Moragh took them to New York's Penn Station and deserted them! Peter was five and Michael was two. The English Speaking Union contacted Chasey and the boys were placed in separate foster homes. Peter did well, but sensitive Michael was deeply scarred.

It is a mystery how in wartime she was able to board a ship and return to England. Soon after her return, Jack filed for divorce…infidelity.

The war ended and Peter and Michael sailed home to be reunited with their father. He worked with the Marshall Plan Project — America's way to help rebuild Europe. But his work was in Germany. Therefore the boys lived with an aunt, and eventually went to boarding school. As an adult, Peter said, "When we returned from America, we had lost our mother and all we ever wanted was to be with Father." That only came about a number of years later.

Over the years of knowing Chasey, she regaled me with stories of my ancestors, going back to 1639, when Aquila Chase landed in Massachusetts. Some of it was a bit unbelievable, some documented. I was anxious to learn my more about my family history.

The plane got chilly so I pulled my sweater tight around my shoulders. The flight was halfway over. Soon I would be seeing someone with eyes that might be like mine or our mother's. I put thoughts of my birth mother out of my mind and instead pictured the bright eyes of my own three children. I never could have given them up.

Moragh and her detrimental choices were far reaching—affecting many lives. I was confident that the Lord put it on my heart to find my sister. He was guiding my every step, sometimes in miraculous ways.

He never abandons His children.

**Moragh by Chasey**

# 11

# Family life

Meeting my grandmother proved to be an exciting milestone. After our informative visit with her in Albany, we returned to our apartment, family, and friends. Jim was busy with his career at IBM and our new married life was good. We were very close.

Our friends George and Betty Orteig asked us to babysit their infant son. (George's grandfather had given the $25,000 reward to Lindbergh for his solo flight to Paris). After a quiet evening, it occurred to us that a baby might complete the picture. I had never been around babies, I didn't know how to hold, change, feed, or rock them to sleep. How hard could it be? A few hours with our neighbor's baby had been a breeze!

What did *we* know?

Soon I was pregnant, and ten days after our first anniversary, we welcomed Marjorie Vivian. We called her Mivy. The first time I picked her up, her head bobbled and I was afraid I had broken her neck! This was just the beginning of learning what it meant to be a Mommy.

Miss Burton, our Scottish nurse came every day for a month. She was calm, kind, and gentle. She gave Mivy the start she desperately needed. When she left, reality set in. This was not a breeze for the nervous novice.

When Mivy was a few months old, we decided to hire a babysitter for our first evening out. Other parents in Peter Cooper recommended the student nursing service at nearby Bellevue Hospital. They would send a qualified nurse right to our door.

We anxiously awaited the arrival of the student who would care for our first born. The doorbell rang, Jim opened the door and there stood a young black man. With confidence he said, "I'm your babysitter."

"The hell you are!" Jim replied as he tried to close the door.

I backed away and left the two of them to reach a resolution. The young man didn't seem offended by Jim's reaction. With a broad smile and polite manner he said, "My name is Jim Arrington." I eavesdropped as he won over my husband. Our door opened wide and Jim Arrington entered our apartment—and ultimately, our lives and our hearts.

He had wanted to be a physician, but couldn't afford medical school because he had already put his brothers and sisters through school. He was brilliant and a member of Mensa. He was a talented, polite, loving, wise friend—a gift from God. A born teacher, he taught us about baby care, how to tango, introduced us to more classical music, and the local restaurants.

When we were expecting our second baby, we took the next step in the "American Dream" and moved to the suburb of Larchmont. Our first house at 9 Hawthorne Road was a little barn red Dutch Colonial. In March of 1953, daughter Diana Stoddard arrived. We called her Dede. The hospital staff was surprised to see Jim Arrington bringing flowers to a white woman! To this day we have stayed in touch. He is a believer and he, too, may have been sent to pray for us.

Suburbia meant the typical suburban lifestyle...Jim commuting to the city, and my staying at home with the children. In 1956, our son John was born. I wanted to name him John Spencer Locke. But my father-in-law John was a stern, highly disciplined man who insisted on preserving family history and traditions. "The Locke men did not have a middle name and for generations the names alternated from James to John." Period! End of discussion. Later research proved he was as good a storyteller as Chasey.

### John and Cora Locke

My father-in-law was a very handsome, distinguished looking man with piercing dark eyes and grey hair. He was a dapper dresser and a pipe smoker. He was a Yale graduate as were many of the Lockes. In his college years he had been a fine athlete. His career began as a broker on Wall Street until the crash, and then he served in the military and later became a hospital administrator.

My mother-in-law, Cora Stoddard Locke, was a beauty with green eyes, auburn hair, and a fun loving disposition. One of her familiar sayings was, "Some people are givers and some are takers." She was a giver. She and John were a stark contrast.

John spent years researching and gathering family antiques. He had the history and a story for each item— furniture, paintings, silver, jewelry, etc. When he and Cora married, she longed for modern furniture..."not all those old things." But she submitted and the "The General" as his family called him, ruled the roost.

When we were first married, they lived in Long Island and were a part of our growing family life. Because of career changes, they spent a number of years in San Salvador and North Africa.

**Jim, Asst. Mgr.**

In Larchmont, we were active in the Newcomers Club. We joined the Orienta Beach Club, where Jim played tennis, I would take the children to the beach, and we would attend dinner parties and dances. Jim left IBM and went into management with New York Life.

We made interesting new friends: Jane and Bobby Nicholson, who played Clarabelle on TV and Doc Severinsen from *The Tonight Show*. He arranged for our Newcomers group to go to a *Tonight* show. That night Jonathan Winters was a guest. Jim and Johnny had been childhood friends in Dayton. After renewing friendships, the Winters family moved to Larchmont and joined Orienta. Johnny practiced some of his new routines on us and other club members.

A dissatisfaction of life began to stir in me: "*If only* my circumstances would change then I would be happy." *If only* I had gone to Parsons. "*If only* things changed" became my way of life. Some of our friends began having trouble with their teenagers. Jim and I saw what might lay ahead for us— *If only* we could raise our children in a better environment.

The dismal grey skies of winter, the cold, the furnace heat, all left me feeling down. Conversations turned to Florida as a few friends had moved there. Sunny blue skies, swaying palms, and orange blossoms sounded wonderful. *If only* we could move to Florida, surely I could be happy there.

In 1956, after Daddy and Irene returned from Europe, he became ill. His doctor had told him to slow down because of heart problems. "I could wrap myself in cotton batting and live to be 100," he said. "But I don't call that living."

We were suddenly called to his bedside and by evening he was gone. He died of an aneurism. I was thankful that I had a chance to say goodbye, but the finality was a dreadful blow...it was my first experience of losing a close family member.

After spending several days at Aunt Kitty and Uncle Ed's home, receiving friends before the funeral, I went back to my life, without daddy—my idol, my friend, my guide.

He had always accepted me as I was and I missed his presence. Having a generous, loving father made it easier for me to later respond to my Heavenly Father.

My mother, much to our dismay, sent a postcard telling me she had eloped in the Caribbean to marry a longtime friend. Her husband Jack Frankland was employed at The Bureau of Standards in Washington. Jack was a brilliant but troubled and displeasing man, who encouraged her drinking and separated her from many of her friends.

With my father gone and my mother far away, there seemed little reason for us to remain in New York. I pressured Jim about Florida until he finally said, "If I found a job I might consider the move." We drove to familiar Sarasota, where brother Bill lived, then to visit friends in Palm Beach, and lastly to Fort Lauderdale. No job offers.

Nearing Orlando, Jim remembered that Bob Carrigan, his University of Virginia roommate, lived in Winter Park. Bob, a realtor "happened" to need an insurance man. They sealed the deal with a handshake.

Selling our Larchmont house, we loaded up the Pontiac station wagon and headed south. Nine-month-old John learned how to stand up halfway through the Lincoln Tunnel! On July 3rd 1957, we arrived in Winter Park. We stayed at Neidert's Court on 17-92 and Lee Road. A cluster of little cabins gave us our first taste of Florida — tiny ants and big roaches!

The first house we purchased was on Mizell Avenue. Mivy, now called Margie, entered first grade at Park Avenue Elementary. Her classmate Nancy's parents, Ken and Lee Moar, became our first and best friends. We had cook-outs, played bridge, and vacationed together. The men fished, and Lee and I had numerous creative projects in the works, including sewing clothes for the girls and ourselves.

I wanted to give our children what I didn't have as a child — exposure to the spiritual aspect of life which we thought would be found in a Winter Park church.

**New Florida Home**

My *If only* was not through with me yet. It has been said, "You can get away, but you take yourself wherever you go."

# 12

# Searching for the Answer

I had what I wanted — Florida and a new beginning. Our children had a simpler environment, Jim was working, and we were involved in our community. I thought things were happier because of the sunny climate, and easy lifestyle. Instead it was God working behind the scenes. He loved me enough not to leave me where I was — either physically, emotionally, or spiritually.

Two things began to sink in...Jim left a better career in New York and yet moving did not fill my emptiness. "Is this all there is?" Discontent clouded everything. I even began seeing Jim in a negative light. Maybe parting our ways would solve *my* problems.

Jim wanted to work things out so we went for marriage counseling, but psychiatry was not the answer! We explored divorce. Confused, I felt compelled to pray. Wasn't that done in church? The nearest church doors were locked. God was aware of my needs. While I stumbled about, He walked beside me, quietly wooing me by His Spirit.

*"You saw me before I was born and scheduled each day of my life before I began to breathe" (Psalm 139:16).*

A friend said, "Nina, one day you will look back and see that God had a reason for your problems." I thought she had been out in the sun too long! Her words haunted me, echoing in my mind over and over! Was God really concerned with my life?

During that dark time of indecision, Jim and I went to Fairway Market. We still needed to eat even if our lives were falling apart. As we left the store, Jim stepped between two cars. Realizing one of the cars was backing up; he suddenly dropped to the ground to avoid being crushed. My heart cried out, "He could have died!"

God used that near accident to open my eyes and turn me around. I loved this man and couldn't bear the thought of life without him. My self-absorbed emptiness would not be filled by leaving Jim. Healing slowly began. We didn't know that it was the grace of God keeping us together.

The following year we moved to 409 Langholm Drive. We wanted a bedroom for each child and a neighborhood with playmates. Build a pool and they will come! One summer Chasey visited us and what joy she had with the grandchildren she never dreamed of knowing. They sat at her feet listening to her adventures and her childhood stories of *Speckledy Hen*.

In 1960, I flew to New York to accompany Chasey to the dedication of the new Chief Medical Examiner's building. Chasey and I huddled together under an umbrella in the rain listening intently to every speaker. The event began with the National Anthem, then the invocation by Cardinal Spellman, Archbishop of New York. Dignitaries included the Governor, Senator Javits and Mayor Wagner. We heard of the importance of forensic medicine, and how new facilities would expand their work.

The blue-and-white glazed brick exterior rose at the corner of First Avenue and 30th Street. District Attorney Dr. Hogan commended Dr. Helpern for his dedication to many years of service as CME. Helpern, a quiet and humble man, was touched but embarrassed by the accolades he received.

After the ceremony, he drew Chasey aside to tell her how he appreciated her and that her 7'x 10' mural "The

Autopsy" would be displayed in the new building. What a blessing to share this meaningful day with my grandmother.

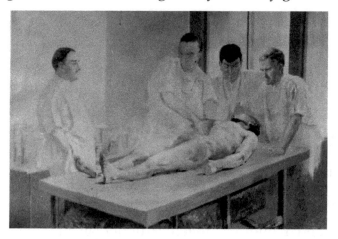

**Unfinished Drawing by Chasey**

Afterwards, we went to the apartment of cousins John and Anne Brownell. Their son John wore the MacColl kilt for us. I met cousin Tids, a decorator at B. Altman's and close friend of Chasey's. She had a wealth of MacColl family history.

Returning to Princeton, we had lunch at Grace and Gerry Lambert's home. Gerry was President of Lambert Pharmaceutical. As avid art collectors for years, their house was filled with an extensive art collection including Degas, Van Gogh, Turner, Renoir, and others.

Nothing satisfied me for long. Our close friends the Dickinson's bought a lovely estate on a lake. *If only* we had a bigger house.

We found such a house at 1508 Park Avenue. Built in 1882, the two-story white frame home surrounded by old oak trees, sat on four acres in a citrus grove. Two brick columns stood by the road forming a gracious entry. We called our new home Loxwood, the name of an old English manor.

The first evening we entered our new home, I had a feeling of doubt and fear. The old house needed work from top to bottom. What had *I* done? Were we up to the challenge physically or financially?

In 1960, there were no home inspections. That winter brought a record-breaking freeze. The furnace had a hole in it so we were without heat. Our family huddled by the fireplace in blankets and gloves to keep warm. The fruit trees dropped all their fruit and leaves, leaving a rotten mess that had to be bulldozed away. My *"If only"* — like London Bridge — was falling down.

We renovated one room at a time for twelve years, doing much of the work ourselves. Our contractor Charlie Chapman was there so often, he was considered one of the family.

The living room had a lovely old fireplace and mantel. We scraped off the old grass cloth and painted the walls soft yellow. Under the old carpet there was only plywood. To look original, we covered the floor with dark stained eight-inch wide oak plank. Yellow linen drapes hung at the windows with original blown glass panes.

A small fireplace warmed the cozy library. I filled shelves with old leather books from garage sales. Upholstery and curtains were covered in golden French Toile.

We installed an antique marble mantel from New Orleans in the guest room. The wallpaper was a Damask pattern. I discovered a butterflied-walnut headboard for $2.50 to add to grandmother Vivy's French antique pieces. An upholstered chair was covered with my newest hobby — needlepoint. It was appropriate that my mother was our first guest.

At a used furniture shop, we found a solid walnut buffet for $12. A brass and crystal chandelier hung over a $100 cherry dining room table that seated twelve. Matching wall sconces lit up the yellow floral reproduction wallpaper.

On cool evenings, our family relaxed on wicker furniture or a swing on the front porch. One of us would throw an orange into the grove for our dog Muffin to retrieve. He bounded like a gazelle with his ears flying straight out from his head.

We closed in the back porch to make a "great room," a new concept at the time. A pool table and comfortable furniture made it a place for many gatherings. The master bedroom had a fireplace and dumbwaiter.

As a surprise on Margie's thirteenth birthday, she returned from school to a newly decorated bedroom—just as my parents had done for me. Then, on Dede's thirteenth birthday, while sleeping, Jim lifted her out of her bed and we transformed her room. The next morning, she awakened to a new décor. Jim and I loved renovating places together and making a "silk purse out of a sow's ear." But renovations only satisfied me temporarily.

In the '60s, we were concerned with the educational system and the direction of our country. We entered politics as precinct workers and campaigners for candidates. I was elected Republican State Committeewoman, and a Barry Goldwater delegate to the '64 Republican Convention.

Politics could take every waking hour if we let it. We left the children many evenings, but made sure they had "dinner" — usually Spaghetti-Os. Margie's response was she would never go into politics! "Never say never." When she was elected Winter Park Commissioner, I presented her with a can of Spaghetti-Os!

As our children reached their teens, rebellion became a problem in our home. I expected our children to measure up to my standards. No wonder they rebelled. Yet the deepest longing of my heart was to be a good mother. I often lost my patience. Each day I would say to myself, "I am going to be patient today." But I didn't have the *power* to be the kind of wife and mother I wanted to be. The battle was my undoing...and the beginning of one of the best things that ever happened to me.

# 13

# The Choice

In 1958, the Lockes and the Moars joined the Congregational Church. We gave little of ourselves, and received little in the way of spiritual teaching. But after a major disagreement at a meeting, we began looking for a new church home.

Jim's background was Presbyterian, we married in a Presbyterian church, and my unbelieving father's funeral was in a Presbyterian church. So for those "good spiritual" reasons, we became Presbyterians.

I then became involved in our new church serving as Missions Chairman. I knew *nothing* of missions or missionaries. At our first Board meeting we gathered in a circle to pray. As an unbeliever I panicked at the thought of praying out loud—my hands were clammy and my heart was pounding. I mumbled something but at least I didn't pray, "Now I lay me down to sleep..." Now seemed to be the right time to buy my first Bible rather than a coffee table version.

I read Genesis, got to the "begats," skipped to the end to see how it all turned out! I gave up. Around that time, I was deeply moved by the movie *Ben Hur*. As the cross was dropped into the ground with a loud thud, I gasped— something was happening inside of me.

Now that I had a Bible, it also seemed proper to buy a manger. Woolworth's in the Colonial Mall had one for $5.95. I felt very uncomfortable after Christmas ended wrapping "Baby Jesus" in brown paper and putting Him in the attic for another year. Later I would come to know that He could be with me always.

I acknowledged that I needed help...our family was slipping away. My demands and criticism were producing dissolution. I went everywhere for answers, but *no one* told me Christ was the answer.

During a Sunday sermon, our minister asked, "Are you a witch in your own home?" *Yes, I am!* At that moment I felt a strong hand on my shoulder. I turned around but no one was there. I had a sense of peace as I let go...somehow, things were going to be alright. Perhaps our minister might guide me. We met and as I poured out my heart to him, he slumped deeper and deeper in his chair. Then quietly said, "Nina, there's a lot of rebellion going around." Isn't that what the doctor says when you have a virus? No prayer was offered, no Biblical counseling given. If a man of God couldn't tell me what I needed, then I was totally *lost*!

I went home, threw myself on the bed, and cried out to God. "I don't know who You are, but I am desperate! If You are there, show me the way."

> *"In the day of my trouble I shall call upon You, for You will answer me"* (Psalm 86:7).

My confused mind even thought, *If only* our family could get away, perhaps Europe, expand our perspective — surely then we could be happy.

I called a travel agency and spoke to Betty Berry. She "happened" to know a family just returning from Europe. "Let's have lunch with Mary Jane Morgan and she can tell you about their trip." I wasn't the least bit interested, but I smiled and said, "Yes." Hadn't I just asked God to show me the way? His hand of *providence* was moving on my behalf. I was unaware that Mary Jane had prayed with her Bible teacher, Marty Mandt, before our lunch and was prepared to share the gospel with me. Looking at my appearance she determined that I had it all together and would not be interested. I was wearing my mask while crying inside for help.

At lunch, Betty mentioned the Bible class. I thought that's one avenue I haven't tried. I took out my notepad and wrote down the information—they met at the YMCA on Mills Avenue. The following Tuesday I was there. Pat Billings led a small group through the Campus Crusade for Christ booklet called *The Four Spiritual Laws*. After years of God tenderizing my heart, on January 28, 1969, I prayed to receive Christ into my life. I knew immediately that I was a new creation, old things had passed away. I couldn't express it or explain it. Christ had changed the core of my life.

The next week, Jane McKeller took us through *The Spirit Filled Life* booklet. She shared Dr. Bill Bright's principle of *Spiritual Breathing*. He and his wife, Vonette, founded Campus Crusade for Christ. Spiritual breathing revolutionized my everyday living! When I lost my temper, or was unforgiving—the moment sin entered my life—I confessed it, turned from it, and thanked God for His forgiveness. I surrendered control of my life and by faith relied on the Spirit to fill me with His presence and power. Circumstances no longer had control over me. I could live a victorious life in the power of the Holy Spirit.

Mary Jane became my mentor. I attended Marty Mandts' Bible class every week, responding to her verse-by-verse practical Biblical teaching. Marcia Voorhis, a political friend, attended the class and I was glad to renew our friendship. After class many had lunch together, made new friends, and heard about what Christ was doing in their lives.

> *"He chose us in Him before the foundation of the world...In love He predestined us for adoption as His sons through Jesus Christ"* (Ephesians 1:4-5).

At age thirty-nine, I discovered I had been adopted not once, but twice. Everyone desires to be wanted—to be in a relationship. First, God filled my need to belong to an earthly family. Then having chosen me from ages past, God in His extravagant grace drew me into His family through His Son. Now I belong to a second family—the family of God, both here on earth and for all eternity.

Below is a copy of the message shared with me the day I received Christ. Originally titled *The Four Spiritual Laws*, now called *How to Know God Personally*.

### How to Know God Personally

What does it take to begin a relationship with God? Devote yourself to unselfish religious deeds? Become a better person so that God will accept you?

You may be surprised that none of those things will work. But God has made it very clear in the Bible how we can know Him.

The following principles will explain how you can personally begin a relationship with God, right now, through Jesus Christ...

### Principle 1:

God loves you and offers a wonderful plan for your life.

### God's Love

"God so loved the world that He gave His one and only Son, that whoever believes in Him shall not perish, but have eternal life." 1

### God's Plan

[Christ speaking] "I came that they might have life, and might have it abundantly" [that it might be full and meaningful]. 2Why is it that most people are not experiencing the abundant life? Because...

### Principle 2:

All of us sin and our sin has separated us from God

### We Are Sinful

"All have sinned and fall short of the glory of God." 3

We were created to have fellowship with God; but, because of our stubborn self-will, we chose to go our own independent way, and fellowship with God was broken. This self-will, characterized by an attitude of active rebellion or passive indifference, is evidence of what the Bible calls sin.

### We Are Separated

"The wages of sin is death" [spiritual separation from God]. 4

This diagram illustrates that God is holy and people are sinful. A great gulf separates us. The arrows illustrate that we are continually trying to reach God and the abundant life through our own efforts, such as a good life, philosophy, or religion -- but we inevitably fail.

*The third principle explains the only way to bridge this gulf...*

**Principle 3:**

Jesus Christ is God's only provision for our sin. Through Him we can know and experience God's love and plan for our life.

### He Died in Our Place

"God demonstrates His own love toward us, in that while we were yet sinners, Christ died for us." 5

### He Rose From the Dead

"Christ died for our sins...He was buried...He was raised on the third day, according to the Scriptures...He appeared to Peter, then to the twelve. After that He appeared to more than five hundred..." 6

### He Is the Only Way to God

"Jesus said to him, 'I am the way, and the truth, and the life; no one comes to the Father, but through Me.'" 7

This diagram illustrates that God has bridged the gulf which separates us from Him by sending His Son, Jesus Christ, to die on the cross in our place to pay the penalty for our sins.

*It is not enough just to know these three principles...*

## Principle 4:

We must individually receive Jesus Christ as Savior and Lord; then we can know and experience God's love and plan for our lives.

### We Must Receive Christ

"As many as received Him, to them He gave the right to become children of God, even to those who believe in His name." 8

### We Receive Christ Through Faith

"By grace you have been saved through faith; and that not of yourselves, it is the gift of God; not as a result of works, that no one should boast." 9

### When We Receive Christ, We Experience a New Birth

### We Receive Christ by Personal Invitation

[Christ speaking] "Behold, I stand at the door and knock; if any one hears My voice and opens the door, I will come in to him." 10

Receiving Christ involves turning to God from self (repentance) and trusting Christ to come into our lives to forgive our sins and to make us what He wants us to be. Just to agree intellectually that Jesus Christ is the Son of God and that He died on the cross for your sins is not enough. Nor is it enough to have an emotional experience. You receive Jesus Christ by faith, as an act of the will.

These two circles represent two kinds of lives:

### Self-Directed Life

Self is on the throne, directing decisions and actions (represented by the dots), often resulting in frustration. Jesus is outside the life.

### Christ-Directed Life

Jesus is in the life and on the throne. Self is yielding to Jesus. The person sees Jesus' influence and direction in their life.

Which circle best describes your life?

Which circle would you like to have represent your life?

The following explains how you can receive Christ:

You can receive Christ right now by faith through prayer

Prayer is talking to God. God knows your heart and is not so concerned with your words as He is with the attitude of your heart. The following is a suggested prayer:

*"Lord Jesus, I need You. Thank You for dying on the cross for my sins. I open the door of my life and receive You as my Savior and Lord. Thank You for forgiving my sins and giving me eternal life. Take control of the throne of my life. Make me the kind of person You want me to be."*

If this prayer expresses the desire of your heart, then you can pray this prayer right now and Christ will come into your life, as He promised.

Does this prayer express the desire of your heart?

Yes, I just asked Jesus into my life or

I may want to ask Jesus into my life,
but I have a question I would like answered first.


Scriptures to answer your questions:

(1) John 3:16 (NIV); (2) John 10:10; (3) Romans 3:23; (4) Romans 6:23; (5) Romans 5:8; (6) 1 Corinthians 15:3-6; (7) John 14:6; (8) John 1:12; (9) Ephesians 2:8,9; (10) Revelation 3:20.

Adapted from *Have You Heard of the Four Spiritual Laws* and *Would You Like to Know God Personally*, by Dr. Bill Bright, co-founder of Campus Crusade for Christ. © Campus Crusade for Christ. All rights reserved. Used by permission from Bright Media Foundation 11/1/12.

# 14

# The Trial and Joy of Being Made New

The change began to show. Dede told her dad, "It's just another one of mom's phases. She'll get over it." I had taken up causes, classes, politics, and renovated old houses. I began doing needlework, changed churches, and strived to be a patient mother. None of which filled the emptiness— "my God-shaped vacuum." All my endeavors failed. I finally learned I was unable to change myself, but God was able to by the power of His Holy Spirit.

I had an urgent desire to share what I had discovered with the man who had patiently loved me through all these phases. I prayed that Jim would begin a personal relationship with Christ.

I planted books and tracts throughout the house, and suggested (or urged him) to accompany me to Christian events. I was like a Billy Graham surrogate but Jim was confused by the new me.

One day as I begged him to come to a Bible class, he turned with those piercing brown eyes and said emphatically, "Woman, get off my back! I'm a sinner and that's the way I intend to stay."

Shocked by his response, I quickly called Mary Jane. "What do I do now?" She said, "Now honey, do exactly as Jim said—back off. Forget the class, fix him a nice dinner, and be the loving wife God intends you to be. Stop trying to get him to read books and go to meetings. It is the work of the Spirit to draw him. You just love him to the Lord." That sounded easy. However, there were many struggles in resolving to stand firm on God's truth.

Four months later, my husband accepted Christ and we became one in Him. Over the following years, we were a team: sharing our faith, counseling young couples, discipling others, and giving our testimonies. Everything that had been good in our marriage was that much better when we learned to abandon ourselves and rely on the Holy Spirit living in us.

Within a few weeks, God personally revealed Himself to Jim in an amazing way. At our first weekend retreat, Marty Mandt said, "Jim, I understand you are trying to quit smoking. If so, how often do you light up a cigarette?" His answer (exaggerating) was, "Every five minutes."

Marty suggested that he pray and ask the Lord to take away the desire to smoke for five minutes. Then in advance, thank Him for taking the desire away. Jim asked for the first five minutes and never had the desire to smoke again! God became very real to my Jim that day.

I had been the decision maker in our home. As believers we learned that the man was the head of the home and the woman was his helpmeet (partner) so we began a major flip—when our children asked to go somewhere or do something, my retort was, "Go ask your father." There was confusion at first but as we were faithful, the Spirit enabled us to redirect our priorities resulting in new family harmony.

One Sunday after church, Jim asked the children what they learned in Sunday school. John piped up and said, "I learned how to make a martini—bottles and all!" It was true! What were we as new believers to do? Someone suggested we write to Ben Haden, a Presbyterian minister in Chattanooga. Three weeks later, he called our home. During the conversation he said, "If Christ returned next week, is this where He would want to find you and your family? Find a church where the Bible is taught and Christ is honored." We did.

God was also moving in the lives of our three children. Kelly Whitaker, the daughter of one of my Bible study friends, invited Dede to go to a Campus Crusade meeting at the Winter Park Youth Center. It was there that she gave her life to Christ. John also saw the change in me, saying, "Mom, the wicked old witch really is dead." He went to Camp Westminster and gave his heart to the Lord. Margie went to Mount Vernon College in D.C. When she returned home that summer, she had no plans to return to school. She began to reveal some of her struggles. Jim and I had already claimed some of God's promises for Margie.

As Margie talked, I listened, loved her and silently prayed for God's wisdom. "Mom," she said, "You're not crying or yelling. What has happened?" I said, "God is changing me from the inside." She responded, "If Jesus is enough for you, then He's enough for me." At that moment, our relationship began taking steps of understanding and love, rather than those of control and anger.

That fall, our whole family was baptized by Pastor Wagner at Faith Baptist Church in Orlando. I chose my favorite verse to quote at my baptism:

> *"Therefore, if anyone is in Christ, he is a new creation.*
> *Old things have passed away; behold, behold all things*
> *have become new"* (II Corinthians 5:17).

Our family still faced challenges, disappointments, and consequences of wrong choices. The difference was giving thanks and walking in the power of the Holy Spirit through it all. I no longer had to be overwhelmed by my circumstances. As a family, we knew we could face life's challenges by abiding in Christ.

> *"Remain in Me and I will remain in you...I am the vine;*
> *you are the branches"* (John 15:4, 5).

The women's Bible study grew into a weekly couples' group, meeting in various homes. We invited friends, beginning with Ken and Lee Moar, and they too became followers of Christ. Once a month, we invited new people to the group for a covered dish dinner. In a short time the group grew to over ninety people. Orlando was hungry for God.

Jim and I had many Christian gatherings in our home. We hosted several New Year's Eve parties with the Moars.

The group gathered to pray in the New Year while the horns blew outside. Some visitors came out of curiosity, others were seeking, and some met the Savior.

Time passed and our family changed as well—there were graduations, colleges, weddings, and grandchildren were born. These were all fulfilling times, yet a longing filled me to search for someone I had often thought of but had never known. God was leading me to find my sister.

# 15

# The God of the Impossible

The plane moved ever closer to Manhattan and to the culmination of my quest. I leaned back in my seat, closed my eyes to recall the time that I had decided to find Barbara. Perhaps it was the influence of television shows in the seventies with long-lost relatives being reunited. Perhaps middle-age reminded me that time for such endeavors would sooner or later, come to an end.

My journey took me to the newly formed Adoptees Liberty Movement Association – ALMA, which is the Spanish word for "soul." The founders believed that not having the truth about one's origin left a scar on the soul. They had a registry for adoptees and fought for their rights to find their birth families. They told me that the first door to

Barbara was to locate our birth mother. That was not my desire, but I followed their advice. In England, we hired a private detective, but he found nothing.

From 1978 to 1980, I contacted adoption agencies, wrote letters, traveled—all to no avail. Amidst endless hours of investigation and waiting, God began to open doors. With Jim's support and prayer, I felt we were getting closer.

My adoption, arranged directly with Chasey was private, yet my parents had gone through the Child Adoption Agency to be certain there would not be any future legal problems. I went to the agency in New York and spoke with Miss Lillian Sykes. She told me they had no information about my mother or any siblings.

My little white-haired grandmother had told me how to contact my half-brother, Peter in England. We corresponded, but he too knew nothing of his mother or sister Barbara.

In September of 1978, Jim and I turned our path in a new direction—we went to Chase's Mills, Maine–the community of my ancestors. Maybe we would find a clue or perhaps even some of Chasey's paintings. She had given me a drawing of the Chase "Coat of Arms." The motto said, *"Those who are wise – the people of God – shall shine as brightly as the sun's brilliance, and those who turn many to righteousness will glitter like stars forever"* (Daniel 12:3).

She had told us stories of her father, Jeb Chase, who fought in the Civil War. So on our way to Maine, we visited Petersburg, Virginia. There were two items Chasey had donated at her death in 1967, on display in the Quartermaster Museum at Fort Lee. His sword was engraved on the blade, below the thumb bonnet: Lieutenant Jeb Chase 1831. His copy of *The Thirty-Second Maine* by Henry Clarence Houston was also on display.

Our next stop was Concord, Massachusetts to see Nancy and Roy Henderson. They provided a major piece of our puzzle. We were previously unable to locate Chase's Mills on any map or through the postal system. Roy "happened" to have a very old map and there it was! The Lord was going before us, providing once again.

Chase's Mills consisted of three houses and four barns. We recognized my great-grandfather, Solon Chases' house by a photo Chasey had given me. The owners told us that

Kip Chase lived across the road. As Kip walked out of his barn, I extended my hand saying, "I'm Nina, but my grandmother called me Denia."

Tears filled his eyes. "Denia," he said, "I never thought I'd see you again."

Kip, my cousin, remembered me! This was so much more than we had ever expected. We talked for hours in his kitchen around his wood stove in what they called the "Old Squire's house" built by Issac. Kip, like Chasey, had a bubbly personality—full of energy and a zeal for life. He loved to dance, put on his silks and race trotters, or lead local parades driving his horse-drawn wagon. Kip worked his land and had the job of postman. He regaled us with many stories—beginning with *mine*.

Chasey, Moragh, and I came to Chase's Mills in July 1931. Kip still had a vivid picture of me in a sun suit on a leash at Solon's. Kip's parents, Stella and Otho, wanted to adopt me but were unable to because of the Depression. My picture sat on their piano for years. My life would have been very different had I stayed in Maine. We visited Otho, at age ninety in a nursing home, and he remembered little Denia.

**Otho by Chasey**

His son Otho had a daughter Paula, whom we met years later. She had cared for Kip when he was older and she and her husband Scot Burgess still live on the hill above the "Old Squire's house." How I met cousin Paula is another *providential* incident. My friend Betts Willingham met Vera Witt at church. "Where are you from?" she asked. "A small town in Maine" she said. Betts said she only knew of one place in Maine, Chase's Mills. "That's where I am from!" She spoke of her niece Paula Chase. As a result of this *providential* encounter, my daughters Dede and Margie and I took trips to meet Paula. She inherited half the Chase land from her Aunt Kay in 1990 and the other half from her Uncle Kip in 1993. Land that belonged to Isaac, Solon, and Otho. Paula told us that on her wedding day, Kip had driven her to Teague's Hill in Otho and Stella's old buggy. She and Scot were dressed in the style of the 1800s.

Kip's sister Kay was a teacher, then had a successful career in the insurance business, and designed knitting patterns for magazines. Those creative genes are so strong!

Kip told me that Chasey and I were to take the train to New York to visit the family who were considering my adoption. Kip, ten, sister Kay, twelve, Otho fourteen along with other family members went to the Buckfield station to say goodbye. Kip recalled putting a penny on the track to  create a flattened souvenir. He kept it as a memento because he knew he would never see Denia again.

As the word spread of my return after forty-seven years, other relatives and friends came by. Cousin Bill Jordan stopped by and brought a portrait of his father painted by Chasey in 1931.

Kay remembered feeding me graham crackers and milk at Solon's. As a teacher, she taught me new words, and hugged me a lot. Nobody knew that Moragh was pregnant again and would have another daughter in February 1932.

My cousins showed us a book written by Jeb Chase and printed in 1875. It told of Jeb's experience in the fierce battle of Petersburg where he was blinded. *Charge at Day-Break: Scenes and Incidents* told of his injuries:

*The bullet struck me near the left temple and came out through the nose at the inner corner of the right eye, throwing out the left eye in its course. On being struck, my first thoughts were that my last hour had come. I did not fall, but staggering and reeling I walked across the trench, the blood spurting before me from my wound. I now lay down, as I thought to die. Capt. Hammond was the first one at my side. "Captain, I must die," were my first words. "Yes, Chase," he replied, "You have got a death shot."*

But my seventeen year old great-grandfather did not die. Impossible as it seemed, he recovered. He heard the voice of Captain Sargent and asked the men nearby to bring the officer to him.

*A moment later he was bending over me. I put out my hand, saying, "I could not die without bidding you good-bye." He took my hand and said, "Why, Lieutenant, you are not going to die. Your wound is not as severe as it looks." [To the men around him] "Pass on your water and*

*whiskey; the boy is faint and weak from the loss of blood."
He poured a canteen of water on my face, and placed
another to my lips and told me to drink. I struggled and
begged to be allowed to die in peace. Several of the
bystanders told the Captain he was doing wrong to hold
out false hopes to me. He applied the water freely, and at
his command I drank the whiskey. Under the Captain's
treatment the blood from my wound ceased to flow as
rapidly and I rallied a little. By the aid of a penknife he
now extracted some loose pieces of bones projecting from
my nose into my remaining eye. At the same time he said
cheerfully, "I want to save that eye, for it is a great
blessing to have one if you can't have two." These
encouraging words inspired a new hope within me,
although coming from only one of the many around me.
Life at the tender age of seventeen years was dear to me,
and with the Captain's encouraging words I eagerly
grasped for it, and when thus having my mind averted
from death to a prospect of life before me, I was
overwhelmed with pleasure.*

Two of Jeb's superiors carried him on a blanket through
enemy fire to take him to a horse-drawn ambulance. He lay
unattended all night in a field hospital. Five days passed
before Jeb arrived in Washington by steamer with only his
sword, bloody clothes, and "a faith that would not die." His
father, Solon Chase, came to find his wounded son and take
him home to Maine. When they tried to board the train, a
woman said, "Don't let that boy on, I can't ride with such a
maimed person!"

Jeb found the strength to recover, and later served the war effort again as First Lieutenant in the Coast Guard at Rockland, Maine. But the time of healing brought more loss for Jeb.

> *On the morning of December 10th, 1872, while proceeding to perform the labors customary to my daily life, I was attacked with severe pain in my eye, which increased through the day. At sunset, while apprehending no serious result from the sudden attack (owing to the fact that I had experienced similar attacks before) all objects began to fade from my vision. A physician was summoned, but before he reached all nature was to me a blank. I had looked upon my wife and little ones for the last time. Gradually they faded from my view into darkness. While gazing earnestly at the little group, the little three-year-old girl held up her doll, saying, "Pappa, can you see my dolly." I put out my hand to draw the child to me, but all had now vanished.*

Jeb led a good life even after total loss of his sight. He had more children, including my grandmother. Even though his world had become dark, he hoped by example to bring light to others. At regimental reunions of the Thirty-second Maine, he was well known as a "man of good cheer."

Many stories were told and written of my great-great grandfather, Solon Chase—writer, publisher, politician, and presidential candidate. Joe Perhem—a teacher, minister, and square dance caller—gave public recitations from Solon's many speeches. He gave us a private reading, speaking

Solon's words with his heavy Maine accent and inflections. It was as if I was a spellbound little girl sitting at the feet of my famous great-great-grandfather and hearing his words of wisdom. I wish I had my recorder that day!

Solon was described as one of the most engaging, humorous, and convincing public speakers. He had the quaint mannerism of the pioneer Yankee: a rough and ready delivery, a keen logical mind, master of facts and figures that held audiences spellbound. Considered shrewd, but kind, "plain homely," and a great debater—a man of strict integrity, he strongly defended his views. He was a proud, direct descendent of Aquilla Chase. He had the vernacular of a backwoods man. One of his sayings was, "There's still plenty of authority in the home but it is rapidly changing hands." Timely, not just for Solon's day, but ours as well.

At the age of nineteen, Solon was appointed to West Point, but doctors said he had consumption and would not live long. He said, "I was discharged on their advice, and here I am at eighty-six, still sound and hearty. That shows how much doctors know! They are good fellers if you let 'em alone! I'd like to know where that doctor is buried; I'd do a double shuffle on his grave!" He saw President Tyler in D.C. to see if he could be reinstated, but Tyler turned him down. (He did, however, pay for his hotel room).

### Solon Chase by Chasey

Solon married Anne Philips, and they had four children: Jeb, Isaac, Cora, and Carrol. Politically, he left the Whig party to become a Republican, left them to become a Democrat, and then left them both to found the Greenback Party and be its nominee for President. Solon drove his steers and a hayrack through rural districts making speeches to farmers. He said, "My four year old steers ain't worth a cent more now than when they were yearlings." It was his warning of the impending currency question. His campaign slogan, "Them Steers" was painted on a large board fastened to the hay rack. After campaigning, he nailed the board above his barn door where it can still be seen today.

Kip said Solon often spoke of his "half-breed Injun grandmother," Lois Smith. She was raised by white parents, and then married Isaac, a bounty hunter known as the

"Indian Killer." Lois' dowry was some iron pots and utensils. Isaac refused to give her new ones. After she smashed them against rocks, he didn't have a choice. She smoked daily until she died at the age of 102. "Obviously," Solon said, "It was the 'tobaccee' that killed her." Tales of Lois the Narragansett varied among branches of the family, but we heard the official Solon Chase version. Jim and I went to the State House to see Chasey's portrait of Solon.

Kip lived on 200 acres in the Squire's House, built by Isaac in 1820, using 24-inch hemlock boards. Years later, a 100-foot barn with huge hand-hewn beams was added. It housed horse stalls, space for buggies, farming equipment, and shelter for dairy cows. A family graveyard sat on a knoll in the pasture above. The Squire's headstone was marked with a finger pointing upward, "Yonder is my home." There were many tiny gravestones of children lost in a typhoid epidemic. As of 2015, Isaac's empty house still stands.

**"The Squire" by Chasey**

Jim and I watched Kip bring logs out of the woods on a sled drawn by his two horses (one was blind). He showed us the Sap House, where they tapped the white maple trees from 1860 to 1959. Forty gallons of sap made one gallon of syrup. In the early days there had been a large dairy, saw and grist mills, and Coopers who made barrels and stays. Winters were harsh and there was always work to be done. The Martin River flowed through the land below Teague's Hill, Chasey's sanctuary. She would hike deep into the woods. Surrounded by its silence, she carried her paints— and there she found inner peace.

One morning Kip took me to a raised mound on the "backfield." The local tale was that it was old Indian burial ground. Sitting on top and watching the "mare's tail" clouds slip by, Kip said, "From now on this is Denia's Dome." He would return there occasionally to remember our visit.

I shared with Kip about the change in my life since I had come to know the Lord. He listened intently, and then replied, "I was raised in a moral home with a great deal of love. I worked side by side with my father every minute I was not in school. I never heard my father say a critical word. My mother was the disciplinarian, but I was never spanked. I just responded to and respected my parents."

A good moral life was enough for Kip. I gave him *The Four Laws* and said, "Tell me what you think." He never did. If I hadn't searched for my sister, I wouldn't have met my cousins, learned more family history, or begun to pray for Kip and Kay.

**Scot and Paula**

Kip told of his grandfather who lost his way home in a blizzard. He had followed the stacked rock wall with his hands until he saw the light of the house. To us it illustrated how Jim and I had found our way home to Jesus, the Light of the World.

In 2003 and 2006, my daughters and I returned to meet Cousin Paula. As we walked through the "Squire's house," memories flooded my mind. . . the wood stove, the barn, Kip's silks, the Squire's portrait, the buggy. . . twenty-five years later it was still there! Paula and Scot wanted to move the Squire's house from the road to the meadow, but the State Historical Society was not interested in helping. Paula and Scot have a deep love for their Chase land and its history. Paula said Chase's Mills is "A simple place where the past is always present." They have since built a campground by Martin Stream with rental cottages and a hand-hewn log cabin they brought from twenty-three miles away. Paula loves to renovate!

Since the time of the Squire, there had always been a bench in front of the barn—a place "to set a spell" and get local news from passersby. On our first trip, I sat there with Kip.  However, the path to Moragh still escaped us. That path was not the one which would take me to my destination.

# 16

# Finding Barbara

Our trip to Maine energized our search. I called the State Department hoping to find information about Moragh's passport, and her travels between England and the U.S. Being passed from one department to another, I was finally connected to an employee in the passport office. She seemingly "by accident," gave me Moragh's latest married name—confidential but vital information for us, a slip that might take us closer to finding my sister.

Our friends Julian and Mary Myrick told us that the Salvation Army in Atlanta could locate missing persons. With our new information this could be a possibility. I waited months, assuming this too was a dead end. Though I did not know my path, I knew my *Guide*.

I had kept in touch with Lillian Sykes at the adoption agency, in case there was a breakthrough. New York law required adoption records be permanently sealed so I was unable to obtain identifying information. She did tell me that Shirley had married in 1955 and moved to Europe. Jim and I took that slim clue to the library searching microfilm wedding announcements in the New York Times and the Herald Tribune. We started our search with the month of May because more weddings occur in the summer. It was the proverbial needle in a haystack.

Miss Sykes thought we would begin with January, which was when my sister was married. Assuming we would find her, Miss Sykes called Barbara's stepmother to say, "A sibling is about to find Barbara." The stepmother decided not to relay the message. Barbara's half-brother, a Christian in the family, said she would want to know and should be told.

A few hours later, Miss Sykes called and asked me to send her a letter telling of my family history, hobbies, interests, and education in case my sister "ever" came to the agency. God's perfect timing brought Barbara to New York only a few days after my letter arrived. Hearing of my inquiry, she went immediately to the Agency. After reading my letter and seeing my photographs, she laid them in her lap and said, "That could be *my* life!"

We had both grown up in New York, studied interior design, were fashion models, liked to entertain, cook, renovate old homes, and neither of us was athletic. Family and home were our focus.

Meanwhile in Florida, Jim and I were planning to help Dede move into a house in Largo. Before leaving Winter Park, I had tied up the phone mentoring a troubled friend, thus causing Jim to miss his connection with a client. He was not happy with me because now he would have to return home for his meeting. When he did, he found a phone message from Miss Sykes, asking me to call her.

Dede had a phone but it was not yet in service. Jim was full of excitement when he returned to her house. "Nina, Miss Sykes wants you to call her!" I prayed the message would be about my sister! Suddenly Dede's phone gave a short ping. I picked it up; there was a dial tone! I phoned Miss Sykes who asked, "Are you sitting down? Barbara (whose adopted name is Shirley) has come to the agency, read your letter, and wants to meet you!"

She said Shirley was a private person and would not want any publicity from ALMA. I agreed to wait for her to take the first step. I didn't have a telephone number yet to give her. I took a deep breath and prayed that our first conversation would not be from a telephone booth on a busy highway.

The phone man arrived the next morning to initiate service. I said, "It's already working." "Impossible," he replied...I love that word! Now I had a number for Shirley to call. Talking with her was easy. She was delightful and excited to find that she had an older sister. After years of searching, the "impossible" had come to pass.

Shirley told me prior to her wedding, she had gone to the agency to inquire about her birth mother. A social worker told her there was no information on record. My sister left instructions that if her mother came looking for her, she wanted to meet her. This was never entered into her file. Shirley hadn't thought about siblings. And yet, here I was! We made plans to meet in New York the following week.

The Captain's voice came over the intercom; informing us that we would be landing on schedule. I buckled my seatbelt, and whispered a prayer. I had waited a lifetime for this reunion. Manhattan's skyscrapers came into view as I felt the wheels touch the ground. No more daydreaming. Meeting my sister was now a reality.

My brother Burr met me at the airport and drove me to the place of Shirley's choosing—neutral ground rather than where she was staying. Her friends, the Marshalls, let us meet at their apartment on East 81st Street.

January 26, 1980, at 2:45 I rang the doorbell and Shirley opened the door!

# 17

## Sisters

There we were face to face, flesh and blood, meeting after nearly fifty years. We embraced, shed some tears, and talked for eight straight hours!

We shared our lives — our parents, family, childhood, meeting our husbands, our children, and our love of renovating old houses. There were many similarities. We had even gone to the same French-speaking camp in Vermont! At one time we lived in Manhattan only fifteen blocks apart...we may have passed one another on the street, or been on the same bus. Shirley's Aunt Josephine had told her about Chasey — the portrait artist, fascinating but unorthodox. I gave her a copy of the Chase family tree and photos of some of Chasey's art, with information on our extended family in Maine and England.

She knew nothing of Moragh, our birthmother and showed little interest. The fact that Moragh had been given twelve names wasn't unusual, as Shirley's oldest daughter, Lisa also had twelve names. She said, "It was the proper thing to do when you marry into an Old Italian family."

My sister was studying art in Italy when she met Francois, her husband to be. His mother was French and his father Italian. When I later spoke to Francois, who had remained in Italy, he was so excited that we had found each other. He and Shirley had two sons and two daughters. All were high achievers. Their son, Roberto was an artist like Chasey, Ricardo, was a student who later became a residential designer. Lisa, their eldest daughter was a documentary film maker, and Verdella, the youngest was a stewardess before she married.

**Shirley's family**

Shirley's Aunt Josephine was a well-known antique dealer in Manhattan. Somehow she had a connection with Chasey. Josephine also owned a wallpaper company where my sister worked on some new designs. Her artistic talent eventually led her to create a line of hand-knit Italian sweaters that were sold in New York at Bendel's, Saks Fifth Avenue, and Bergdorf Goodman.

Shirley and I had similar coloring: big brown MacColl eyes, diminutive nose, slim and small-boned frame. Her hair had turned gray early in life. Shirley carried herself beautifully as she had studied ballet for many years.

She lived with the Gertrude Vanderbilt Whitney family before her adoption. Gertrude was a patron of the arts and a sculptor. She started The Studio Club in the city for struggling artists, which later became the Whitney Museum at Madison Avenue and 75th Street. One of those struggling artists was the sculptor Jo Davidson, a close personal friend of my grandmother Chasey. This friendship may have been how my sister spent her first year of life with the Whitneys.

The Whitney's youngest daughter was Barbara, for whom my sister had been named. At fourteen months, Barbara was adopted by a physician and his wife and her name became Shirley. She had a very happy childhood with many opportunities but when she was nineteen, her mother died. As an only child, they were especially close and her death was a painful loss. Her father remarried and three stepchildren joined the family. The doctor and his new wife had a son, Shirley's half-brother. He was the one who years later encouraged the family to tell her about a sibling.

While Pat Marshall prepared dinner, I shared my spiritual journey with Shirley. She listened and then threw up her hands and said, "I know what it means to be 'born again,' my half-brother has tried to convert me. It is wonderful for you Nina, but I don't need it. My intellect keeps me from believing in God."

"There's a difference between religion and having a relationship with God," I explained. The conversation ended. I was sad...had God led us to find each other yet not spend eternity together?

Shirley was adventurous; she liked taking risks. Pat, her lifetime friend said, "Growing up, she was very popular and had many friends. As an only child, she was lonely and insecure." I was familiar with those emotions. She attended Sarah Lawrence in Bronxville and excelled in design, music, and art history—subjects we had in common. During a semester in Italy, Francois saw her, was enchanted and actively pursued her. They were married in Manhattan. In the early years of their marriage, they lived on a feudal ancestral family farm in southern Italy on the Adriatic. Mussolini had taken many of Francois' family properties during WWII. Shirley and Francois' struggles were too great to live on the land that remained so they moved to Rome.

For the few days that Shirley and I were together, I stayed in Bronxville with my brother Burr and his wife Sue. Our first evening, we sat by the fire, talking about the day with my sister. Sleep did not come easily. I was both overwhelmed and grateful to God for finding my sister.

The next day, Shirley and I met at the Metropolitan Museum to see the Austrian Hapsburg collection. She got some design ideas for her sweaters. During lunch, she said, "I hope you don't mind that I am a contessa." Her husband Francois was a count, a descendent of an old Neapolitan noble family.

My Manhattan visit concluded with attending the Armory Antique Show. We were both attracted to the same booths. Two years later, Jim and I were drawn back to the city to see Shirley's son, Roberto's art exhibition at the Emmerich Gallery. Chasey, having had her work displayed at a New York gallery, would love to have known that one of her descendants followed in her footsteps.

# 18

# All Things Work Together

Going to brother Burr's that evening; we had dinner with his friends, Jean and Roger Bishop. Jean was going to Orlando the next day and said, "Wouldn't it be nice if we happened to be on the same flight?"

Later that evening, Burr took me aside to have a serious talk; when I began searching for my sister, I had asked him how he really felt. Initially he had said, "Fine, go for it." Later, he said, "What's the matter with *us*?" After admitting that sounded childish, he wished me the best. He told me that brother Bill was not interested, not then, not ever.

Burr's priority was our mother and he hoped I felt the same way. He asked me, "Would that change if you found your birth mother?" I assured him I was not interested in a relationship with my birth mother. My *only* goal was to find my sister. "Marjorie Spencer is the only mother I ever had."

As a graduate from Columbia with a degree in Sociology, he had been intrigued with human development. Amazed at the similarities between Shirley and me, he said, "I will have to reexamine my thinking on genetics versus environment."

That reminded me of the Psalm:

*"For You formed my inward parts; You knit me together in my mother's womb. I praise You, for I am fearfully and wonderfully made" (Psalm 139:13-14).*

On my last day in New York, I had an appointment with Miss Sykes at the Adoption Agency. Miss Sykes was pleased that our meeting had gone extremely well. Two very thick files sat on her desk—Shirley's and mine! When Miss Sykes left the room, I was tempted to look inside but knew that would be wrong. She showed me a few pages indicating how the agency kept detailed records of me for 51 years— newspaper clippings, my graduation, my debut, engagement...even my Daddy's obituary was documented! By law I was not allowed to see anything else. Until the New York law changes, our files are sealed. Miss Sykes, endangering her job, had been an instrument of God making a rare exception that reunited two sisters. Without the decisions she made, I may never have found Shirley!

Burr took me to his favorite restaurant, Giovanni's, for lunch and then to the airport. As I boarded, Jean Bishop was holding a seat for me! We chatted and then our conversation turned to matters of faith. Together we read *The Four Laws.* "My daughter is a Christian." she said. "But when I read the Bible, I find God's dealing with sin depressing so I give up." I gave her *The Living Gospel of John* to read.

The next day she came to our home for tea. She had read some of John and was anxious to talk to her daughter. She asked, "What about Bible studies and churches? Will I lose some of my friends if I become a Christian? Most people in Bronxville don't even go to church."

I thanked the Lord for bringing us together. It saddened me that for now Shirley's response had not been what I had prayed for. But by His love, He gave me the opportunity to share Him with a new friend who *did* respond. It was not an accident that we were on the same plane. Nothing is random in God's kingdom. I was on the path of His choosing. *"All that happens fits into a pattern for good to those who love Him"* (Romans 8:28).

# 19

# Love Abides

I began to care for Mommy as she had always cared for me. Her husband, Jack had died and she was alone in Washington. She was also unhappy with my decision to follow Christ. One of her letters to me was stained with tears, in which she said, "Those are not tears of joy." One time when she and Gina were together, I was told that both had mocked my faith. In 1978, I shared *The Four Laws* with Gina, who that day had a change of heart and came to know the Lord.

In 1977, Burr and I moved Mommy to a Winter Park assisted living facility. We decorated her room with our furniture and her personal belongings. Her doctor in D.C. had kept her heavily sedated, but our physician weaned her off those pills. She was content in her new surroundings. Jack had isolated her and now she was part of a family again.

She died in November of 1980. Those last years were precious to us. She often spoke of choosing me. However I don't know if she ever put her trust in the Lord.

Gina died that year also. Her passing was tragic—she took her life. She couldn't escape the demons that tormented her in this world, but her decision to follow Christ brought her to a place where there is no sin and peace reigns! When Jim and I saw her in 1978, she said, "I want the peace you two have. I answered, "It is in Christ alone Gina, He is our peace."

Five months after meeting Shirley, she and Francois came to Florida. Our family was anxious to meet them. We did some sightseeing, had family gatherings, our closest friends gave a dinner party for them and Barbara Ball hosted a ladies tea. It was a delight to meet Francois. He was warm, charming, and enthusiastic about our expanded family.

In September of
1980, Jim and I went
to Italy. Shirley and
Francois lived on a
working farm named
Monte Calvo, in
Umbria above the

Tiber Valley. Monte Calvo was a seventeenth century stone
farm house they had restored. Next to it was a medieval
chapel and the ruins of an eleventh century tower.

Their house sat on a hill surrounded by 135 acres of
vineyards, wheat fields, almond and fig trees, olive
orchards, and fields of grazing sheep. It was like a picture
from a romantic Italian movie. They raised and produced
almost everything they ate—pecorino cheese from sheep's
milk, poultry, pigs, sheep's wool for mattresses, comforters,
and wool that she dyed for her sweaters. She had twenty
local knitters in their hillside homes making her designs.
One afternoon, we visited one of them. Shirley gave her
instructions in fluent Italian. A jute sweater needed to be
touched up with an iron, so the woman took her iron off the
fireplace coals and made the repair.

Shirley's house had a heavy tile roof, windows with
wood shutters—no screens, eighteenth century wooden

doors, and walls eighteen inches thick. The interior walls were whitewashed; the floors were terra cotta tile with Sisal rugs. Shirley had furnished their home with family pieces and regional antiques that she had found at flea markets. The kitchen had marble counter tops, copper pots hanging from racks, a corner stone oven, and an armoire to hold their dishes.

Our first lunch was on a covered loggia with a fireplace, geraniums, and beamed ceilings. We had a salad of rice, tomato, salami, and haricot beans from the garden, dressed with olive oil from their orchards. Shirley's adjacent studio was filled with wool and fabrics. They planned to restore other sizable buildings on the property to be used as family homes and rentals.

"I live the way folks here live." Shirley said. "I'm in bed early and up early, working hard all day. I know a lot of Umbrian people who I find are kind, moral, and sensitive. The men and women have their traditional roles and there is no crossing over."

We took a picnic lunch to the Hermitage at Assisi, where St. Francis retired and spoke to the animals. Trees in the garden were 1,000 years old. St. Francis had given away all that he owned in protest to the Church's materialism. He lived a humble life by the teachings of Christ, serving the poor and sick. The church had beautiful blue, rose, green and gold frescoes painted by Ghitto in the 1200s.

Her family dines at nine. At our first dinner, there were 18 of us. They live a life of casual elegance, comfortable yet active. Shirley was a gracious hostess—entertaining with ease, beauty, and efficiency. It is a big job to manage a large farm and out buildings. Seeing their home and lifestyle was a good way to get to know them better. We had bonding times as we worked together in the kitchen sharing recipes and cooking techniques.

We went to a nearby "peasant" home to celebrate the couple's fiftieth anniversary. The husband had been a prisoner for eight years during WWII. While missing, his wife cared for their babies and worked in the fields at Monte Calvo. Returning home, he spent all his savings on restoring the chapel where they had been married.

The celebration was a feast with everything grown or raised on their land—antipasto, pasta baked on wood in a stone oven, pigeon, guinea hen, stuffed duck, vegetables, and ended with cake and champagne. I was touched by the obvious love between nobility and peasantry. Later, 150 folk would join them to dine on a whole roasted pig. As a "special" guest from America, I was offered a hot piece of the pork liver. I couldn't turn it down, but oh, how I wanted to find a potted palm!

Francois drove us to many interesting sites: Perugia with its Etruscan walls from forty B.C., Rome to hear the Pope give blessings in five languages, the hole in the ground where Paul had been imprisoned with little air and light. Yet he penned his letter of joy to the Philippians, *"I have learned to be content....I can do all things through Christ who strengthens me."* (Philippians 4:11,13). We visited Pompeii, Positano with its bright colored houses built into the cliffs, and the Isle of Capri on the azure blue sea. We saw a villa where Lisa, my niece was filming a documentary. The villa's unique fireplace was backed with glass so the sea could be seen through the flames.

We were introduced to many of their friends who were anxious to meet "this new sister." Fascinated by our story, they kept saying, "You must write a book."

We spent time with their four children—Lisa, her husband, Renzo Rossellini, a film producer, Roberto, the artist, Ricardo, a teenager, and Verdella—who could have been my own daughter! I looked exactly like her when I was in my teens. Shirley and I were continually finding more similarities. We even discovered we both had Marie Laurencin etchings and wore diamond and sapphire rings that had belonged to our grandmothers. We were content with family and home yet our lives were different. Her family seemed to lack for nothing—except the abiding, personal love of God, which they supposed they didn't need. Little did any of us know that tragedy would bring Jim and me to share that love and to reach out to my sister's family in their darkest hour.

# 20

# Our Only Hope

When tragedy struck Shirley and Francois' daughter, I stood with my sister as she lived through a mother's worst nightmare. Lisa and her husband Renzo were in a major auto accident in Italy. She had massive head injuries, the doctors in Italy offered little hope. So they flew Lisa to the New York Hospital for more medical opinions and care.

Jim and I arrived at the hospital and Francois said, "Lisa is slipping away." She lay motionless in her bed, her husband at her side. He looked up at us with a pained and pleading expression. She was completely paralyzed, only able to move one eye. Her breathing was labored.

"Christ said, '*For where two or three come together in my name, there am I with them*'" (Matthew 18:20).

God promised to be with us and He didn't want anyone to perish without hearing the gospel. We arrived just as the priest anointed Lisa with oil and gave her the last rites. The large family group prayed the Lord's Prayer together and the priest read some Scriptures.

When the Priest left, Lisa made a loud gasp but then her breathing resumed. Shirley embraced me and said, "You have come at just the right time, dear sister, haven't you?" The story of Esther came to mind, when it was said of her, "*You have come...for such a time as this*" (Esther 4:14).

In Florida, our close friend Howard Powell, member of the couple's Bible study and our church, told me that sometimes people in a coma could still hear you speak. "Tell Lisa about Jesus," he said. I was so fearful to speak of Christ with everyone around. Then Lisa's husband, who spoke very little English, and Francois were the only ones left in the room. "Francois," I asked, "May I pray with Lisa?" He seemed moved as he agreed, and left. *God* had emptied the room.

Jim stood at the end of her bed and began praying. I leaned over Lisa and whispered in her ear: "God loves you with an everlasting love. Christ said, 'I am the resurrection and the life. Whoever believes in me shall never die.' Lisa, take Jesus right now before it's too late." It was the only private moment we ever had.

The family made the decision to take her off all life support. Hope for recovery was gone. The next day we brought food to their apartment and found Shirley alone. "I am too tired to think straight," she said. Later, I peeked into her room and she was reading. Jim, my prayer warrior, began to pray that there would be no interruptions to our conversation.

When Francois had heart surgery a few years before, I had spoken to Shirley about trusting the Lord. "I don't know how to trust the Lord," she said. I told her, "I didn't know how either until someone shared this little booklet with me. It's one of my most prized possessions." Sitting on the edge of her bed, we read *The Four Spiritual Laws* together. She made no comment until I asked her which circle represented her life.

"It's all so simplistic, and I don't believe I'm a sinner," she said. "I live by Christ's teachings." After listening to her objections, I returned to the booklet. When we came to the prayer, she remained silent. "You may not want to pray right now, but I believe one day you will." She nodded, "Perhaps." "When you do, this is what will happen: Christ will come into your life, your sins will be forgiven, and you will have eternal life." I gave her a copy of *God's Promises*. "I wrote some words inside for you." I said.

She tucked the booklet inside the cover and said, "I won't read it now because I would cry. I don't have self-pity about Lisa, but I don't understand why someone so lovely, creative, and intelligent would be snuffed out. I keep reminding myself it was an accident." My prayer for her now would be to ask the Holy Spirit to bring the Scriptures we had read back to her mind over and over again. There is power in His Word. We hugged and said goodbye as we were leaving the next morning. I saw love on her face.

On April 13th, I awakened with a strong impression to pray for all of them in New York. I earnestly prayed "Lord, I intercede on behalf of Lisa. Draw her to Yourself."

That afternoon Shirley called—Lisa had died that morning. I ached for my sister; I could only imagine her grief. But I had hope that Lisa was in heaven. There was a service in New York at Ignatius Arola and a funeral in Rome at Santa Maria. She was buried in the Rossellini tomb.

# 21

# A Surprising Turn

Nearly two years passed as Shirley and I wrote and called each other. One day I received an unexpected letter from the Salvation Army. An officer in London had spoken to the husband of Moragh MacColl Thornycroft informing him of my search.

Where would this lead me? I had found my sister; the need to locate Moragh was over. But her life — abandoned children, failed marriages, estranged from her mother...she must have a heart need and I wanted her to know Christ, the burden bearer. This is what she wrote:

*January 5, 1982*
*Dear Nina,*

*My husband recently received an enquiry from the Salvation Army in London regarding enquiries you had instigated as to the whereabouts of your natural mother.*

*Shattering as this was, and after considerable thought, we feel you are due a reply after all the time and trouble you must have taken.*

*My husband and I have an adopted daughter, now aged 33, and we have had to think of this question of adoptive parents and children questioning the past. We have seen some happy and tragic outcomes of such investigations. Luckily in this case my husband knew of your existence, which softened what might have been a great shock. I do not know how many individuals, or relation, have been involved in this search, but I do not care for the obvious lack of privacy in our private lives.*

*I most sincerely hope your childhood was happy with good parents and that life in general has been good to you in every way.*

*Should you wish to make a reply in a written letter you may write to me as follows.*

*Sincerely,*
*Moragh Thornycroft*

I studied the letter, her beautiful penmanship, and I tried to read between the lines. An adopted daughter, the age of our Margie! The officer indicated her husband was most surprised to hear about me, indicating that she had never told him. I had questions I wanted to ask her, *Who was my father? What was he like?*

I wrote my response:

*February 4, 1982*

*Dear Moragh,*

*Obviously you have been shocked by my inquiry and for that I apologize. I didn't know how the Salvation Army proceeded with locating someone. I am sorry that your husband was told rather than you. My intent is not to interfere in your private life.*

*After our marriage, Jim and I met Chasey and kept in touch until her death. She told us family history and gave us numerous mementos.*

*Jim and I went to Solon's house and we met Kip and Kay Chase who recalled our trip to the Buckfield station. The visit encouraged me to search for my sister by locating you.*

*I had loving and kind parents who gave me many advantages. I married a wonderful man and we had three children. But there was an emptiness deep inside that I tried unsuccessfully to fill with activities.*

*Our marriage became shaky, and there was friction in our home. I tried to be patient, and loving, but I was powerless to be the kind of wife and mother I longed to be.*

*I went to a Bible class and heard that the emptiness could only be filled by Jesus Christ. I asked Him to come into my life, forgive my sins, take my guilt, and make me the kind of woman He wanted me to be.*

*He began changing me on the inside, healed our marriage, and our family drew closer. There will always be problems in life but there is no problem so big that Christ is not bigger still!*

*I wanted to share with you the love, peace, and victory that knowing Christ personally brings...You carried me, gave birth to me, and released me. You gave me physical life-He gave me eternal life. I believe I found you for a purpose.*

*Denia*

I enclosed a copy of *The Four Laws*. Shirley also wrote to Moragh. This was not the last we would hear *about* her.

Five years later, our friends Howard and Betty Carol Powell traveled to England. Through the Salvation Army, Howard requested a visit with Mr. Thornycroft, thinking he might be more open.

This is the response that the Salvation Army provided:

*Mrs. Thornycroft has declined your invitation to meet and she had stated quite definitely that she does not wish to have any contact with her daughter.*

*She states, "I hope I have made my feelings quite clear that for me the past must remain a closed book, and I would hope that in the future I will not be contacted again by you or other interested parties."*

After reading her response, I was disappointed and regretful. Rejected? Yes. Hurt, No, because I was very content with the family God had chosen for me. My desire to find Moragh was only to seek family information.

**Peter, Sally, Michael**

The Powell's met Peter and Michael and heard some of their childhood memories. Michael spoke of his sadness and hurt in America. He had been moved repeatedly to different foster homes "because he cried so much." He lost his prized possession, a tiny black comb Chasey had given him. His only connection with his grandmother still brought tears to his eyes. Howard — an intuitive man — told us, "While telling his story, he saw pain and a darkness in his eyes." He loved music and so the Powell's sent him some Christian recordings. Several years later, Michael died of AIDS. Peter had cared for him during his last months. I regret that I never met Michael.

In 1995, Margie and Bill, Jim and I took a trip to England. I was excited to meet Peter...happy, outgoing, and a bubbly personality that reminded me of Chasey and Kip. His wife Sally, sweet and hospitable, welcomed us into their

sixteenth century home filled with history and antiques. Peter had restored and upholstered many of the pieces. These family genes appear again...the gift of  restoration and design.

They served the typical English Sunday dinner of (my favorites) roast lamb with Yorkshire pudding. Peter and Sally had a charming English garden filled with flowers and vegetables. Both enjoyed studying and taking classes in history, art, and music. We were all very comfortable together.

Peter shared a letter written to his father by a social worker with the English Speaking Union. Jack had notified her that he had divorced Moragh and refused all contact between his sons and their mother.

*Dear Mr. Goldsmith,*

*Your letter of May 25th arrived. Mrs. Bruce informed me of your tragic position. May I express my deepest sympathy for you? I appreciate the fact that you have seen fit to inform us.*

*I have often talked with Mrs. Ethel Chase. She was distressed by her daughter's conduct, a lack of moral stability, and irresponsibility about money matters.*

*I am not a trained psychologist, but I am an amateur student of human beings. I believe your wife is psychopathic, and needs treatment. She is not im-moral but a-moral: a Greek distinction describing a person who is unaware of right and wrong.*

*I developed a liking for Moragh although I believe that she is a borderline case. With treatment she might be cured.*

*Your boys are in the best possible hands. They are in the Middle West with extraordinarily kind well-balanced people of means. They have no children and give your two devoted care. They find Michael quite a problem; Peter none at all. Mrs. Chase and I think Michael is like his mother. No one, not even Mrs. Chase, knows where they are.*

*Mrs. Howard Huston*

# 22

# Times Together

Shirley and I had many visits after that first reunion in February 1980. Jim and I went to New York and stayed at the Lawrence home, close, longtime friends of Shirley's family. We discovered a surprising family connection. Their nephew Howard Payne "happened" to live in Sarasota and was also my stepmother Irene's attorney! As children, Shirley and Howard were as close as brother and sister. After all these years, they were able to reconnect.

On one visit, my sister and I (I love to say that) saw some of Chasey's drawings at the Chief Medical Examiner's Museum. We went to the "Americans in Paris" exhibition at the Metropolitan. We were particularly drawn to it because it was of the era when Chasey would have been there. Also on display were some of Tiffany's works from our own Morse museum in Winter Park, Florida.

We went to a rather new museum, the Neue Gallerie, which was located in the former Fifth Avenue residence of Cornelius Vanderbilt. The Klimt portrait of Adele Bloch-Bauer had recently been purchased and put on exhibition. It had been stolen by the Nazis, who also stole her Jewish identity by erasing her name on the portrait. In an ongoing battle, her niece fought to have it returned. They have since made an exciting movie about this story: *Woman in Gold*.

One evening Pat Marshall invited some of Shirley's close socialite friends for dinner. They were anxious to hear how we had met. As we told our story, once again we heard, "You *must* write a book."

I invited Shirley to Redeemer Church. I thought Tim Keller could reach her intellect, but someone else brought the message. At one point, Shirley's body language told me that she had shut down. Still, gratitude filled my heart as I stood side by side with my only sister hearing God's word and singing hymns. Before I left that day, I left this note for Shirley:

*I wanted you to see the way this generation of intelligent, intellectual seekers are worshiping God. They have a relationship with Him that permeates their everyday life.*

*God is very real to them and they come to worship, learn, interact, and apply God's Word. They give and serve others. It's not stifling rules and regulations or a ritual. It is a personal encounter with a living God. He is real to us. Thank you for being open to worship with me. I hope it gave you a broader view of my faith in Christ and touched your heart in some way. It was a precious gift from you and I shall treasure the time we stood side by side hearing His Word proclaimed.*

In 2009, Dede and I went to France to visit Shirley in Barfleur. It was a three-hour train ride from Paris. Dede napped a bit, but I didn't want to miss a moment of the French countryside with its hedgerows, cottages, and quaint villages. The train quickly passed houses with steep tile roofs, black and white cows, sheep, and wide fields of swaying wheat. My parents had given me a love for everything French—the food, language, furniture, decor, and architecture.

Barfleur was a small tranquil town jutting into the English Channel on the Cherbourg coast. The Eau de Gatteville lighthouse rose from the shore and next to it was an eleventh century church dedicated to those lost at sea. Omaha Beach lay nearby. The boat-filled harbor was surrounded by medieval granite houses. We went daily to market for local produce; flat peaches, fresh sea bass, fresh crusty bread and local butter from black and white cows. We happily picked up sweet delicacies from the Pasteria. In summer, the sun sets at ten and rises at seven.

Over the years Shirley's rheumatoid arthritis had taken its toll. She remained brave, without complaint through pain and numerous surgeries. She still manages to have a surprisingly active life. She is an inspiration to me as I deal with my pain from a broken hip.

In 2003, my sister lost Francois. He was born in Barfleur and buried in the ancient churchyard. Three generations had spent summers at his mother's eighteenth century home on the harbor. When stairs became unmanageable for Shirley, she passed the house on to the next generation and renovated a humble fisherman's cottage.

It was a charming, cozy mix of local furniture, family pieces, and architectural embellishments. Soft white cotton curtains hung at the tall windows. Upstairs, there were pastoral views of cottages, lush gardens and fields. At the back of the cottage was a picturesque walled garden with an olive tree, roses, delphinium, herbs, and poppies. Shirley loves to garden.

One evening as we reminisced, we acknowledged that we were both blessed to have been adopted by such fine families. Shirley got teary when I said, "I believe the *providence* of God brought us together." "I am not religious like you. I believe it was fate," she said. I asked her to define fate, but she did not reply. Once again she said, "My intellect keeps me from believing in God...My intellect will not let me go there." My heart ached for Shirley to know Christ and let Him fill her God-shaped vacuum.

That same year, I began thinking about where I would live as I grew older. In 1996, we were shocked when Jim was diagnosed with Alzheimer's. That was unknown territory. After eventually being Jim's caregiver for almost ten years, I knew I didn't want my children to have the *full* responsibility of my care. With *someday* in mind, Margie and I took a tour of the Winter Park Towers retirement community.

We saw numerous living units. One was a house on a cul-de-sac. Walking in the door, I thought, "This might really work." The house "happened" to be available, because it was declined by those on the waiting list. I had four days to decide. The agent wisely left us alone to get a better look. Margie and I went from room to room...*What about this piece of furniture? Was there enough closet and cabinet space? Enough light?*

Having lost Jim, I had never made such a quick major decision *alone*. "Lord if you want me here, it will still be available." Four days later I took a deep breath and said, "I'll take it!" First, I had to sell my house. Two hours after a broker's open house began I had an offer, but I didn't have peace that this was the right buyer. After much prayer, I turned it down. I was taking a huge risk in a slow market. The following day a realtor brought a client to my house who had a check in her purse to purchase another property. She *providentially* changed her mind and used that check to purchase my house! It sold for the full asking price, cash, as is! Thank you Lord.

My new home was a perfect fit for the furnishings I wanted to keep. Even rugs and window treatments from our previous house fit exactly! God led me in many small ways confirming that this was where He wanted me—right in the center of His will.

Two years after I moved, my sister visited. She attended my church, but did not relate to the message. We had deep political and belief differences, amid all the other commonalities. At dinner, when I prayed for the victims of the Japanese earthquake, to my surprise Shirley offered her prayer also.

We had a fun picnic dinner with Dede and Ken in our Central Park. We enjoyed the concert and soloist until a train came through, horns blowing, brakes screeching, and completely drowning out the music! I said, "Shirley, this is a beautiful picture of small town America!"

I awoke early the next morning and spent an hour in prayer, asking the Holy Spirit to show Shirley her need and draw her to Himself. "Lord, could you give me one more chance to ask: *What if* there is a God who made you and loves you? *What if* it's true that you could know Him personally? *What if* there is life after death?"

The opportunity to ask never happened. She did tell me that she admired how our family loved and interacted with each other. My commitment now would be to pray.

*Lord, I pray your Spirit breaks down her barriers. You alone can penetrate her ingrained unbelief. It's hard to accept that You brought us together for life, but not eternal life. Nothing is impossible with You. There is salvation in no other. I pray that You will redeem Shirley and set her free!*

# 23

# Loving Jim

In 55 years of marriage, there were only two household items Jim could not fix: a washing machine belt and a toilet clogged by a child's toy. It took "Joe the plumber" to end both disasters. For a man who always wore a tie, Jim was extremely handy, and enjoyed our repair and remodeling projects.

**Locke Island - 1910**

He came from "good stock." The family had a legacy in the Adirondacks that began when Thomas Pickering Richards first went there from the South. In the 1800's this section of land was called "Number 4." Thomas' son, Eugene was an English professor at Yale. His daughter, Anna, married Dr. James Locke. They inherited "Locke Island" on Beaver Lake and in 1910, Anna and James built a log cabin "camp." There was no electricity, water, or plumbing. Using her finger, Anna etched a saying into the wet cement of the hearth.

> *The cow is in the hammock. The cat is in the lake. The baby is in the ash barrel. What difference does it make?*

The origin was unknown, but it expressed the attitude of the island—a secluded place where the bustling world was left behind to have time to reflect on things that really mattered. When the Market crashed in 1929, James invited several men to the island who had virtually lost every earthly possession. The island peace rescued them and redirected their perspective.

Jim's grandfather, James, settler of this family "camp," was a Yale professor, and editor of the *Baltimore News*. At their Baltimore home, he dressed in black tie every night for dinner. When he came to the island, his Brooks Brothers suit went in the closet, he stepped into the trousers he had left on a chair the previous summer, and put on his sweatshirt. Before returning to the city, he donned his suit and tie and rowed across the lake in his favorite guide boat.

Anna and James had only one son, John, who spent his childhood summers on the island; fishing, canoeing, hiking and playing hunter in the woods. He passed that outdoor life on to his only son, my Jim, whose summers were filled with adventure. He too would grow into a man who wore Brooks Brothers suits in the *real world*. When John's mother Anna died, he inherited Locke Island along with his aunt "Babs." Years later he sold his share to Babs and upon her death it was sold to the Bell family. Jim's parents honeymooned at the cabin and when we were engaged, Jim asked me (his city bride-to-be), "Would you like to honeymoon at Number 4?" I said," No, the Cloisters is more my cup of tea."

On Jim's seventieth birthday in 1995, I surprised him with a trip to Number 4. We didn't know how we would get to Locke Island or what we might find. To our surprise, we met cousin Gertrude Embree, who provided a boat to cross the lake. Jim's eyes glistened as he caught the first glimpse of his grandparent's cabin. He saw many of their furnishings: books, a "Pig Yoke" swing, even the bed he had slept in as a boy! With delight, I watched him as he relived many boyhood memories. The owner, Nan Bell, was glad to welcome Jim's return after 50 years. She had faithfully kept the camp much as it was, had learned of its history, and treasured it.

Number 4 was unique. A large contingent of people came there from Dayton, Ohio. They were entrepreneurs, CEOs, PhDs, leaders in aviation and industry like NCR, the largest manufacturing company in the world, and Mead Paper Company. They left comfort and ease to ride on dusty pitted roads to summer in cabins or "shanties" without facilities—to be away from the "maddening crowds." To hunt, fish, teach their children about wild animals, how to paddle a canoe, and—most of all—take in the solitude and beauty of God's creation. What a heritage for generations to come!

**Cabin in the sky**

Jim gave his family special memories too. In 1965, near Boone, North Carolina, we bought fourteen acres to start our own Number 4 and make memories for our next generations. We built a Jim Walters "log cabin" shell and roughed it for many summers without electricity, running water, or plumbing—just like Number 4. We cooked on a Coleman stove, filled water jugs from town, slept in sleeping bags, and bathed in a metal tub. The five of us cleared trees, dug up stumps, and burned the debris. We had a boat toilet on our deck—the kind that used blue bags and rubber bands. One night Jim went to use the "bathroom." There was a loud crash! The blue bag had not been secured. We cringed...waiting for an angry outburst. Silence...then Jim's contagious laughter echoed through the hills. "Tomorrow," he said, "I'm going to dig a latrine."

He nailed a limb for a seat across two trees and dug a hole. Margie asked, "What about toilet paper?" Upon request, he built a little house with a shingle roof. A builder working nearby thought it was a bird house. It still hangs on the tree.

Church was an important part of our lives. We couldn't all bathe on the same day so we didn't dare go to town in our grubby condition. Instead we held our own service on the deck of our "Cabin in the Sky." Margie drew the bulletin, Dede led the singing, John passed the plate, Jim gave the message, and I made Sunday lunch.

It was better than building a turn-key cabin because roughing it and working on it over the years was an adventure that gave us memories that will never fade. Like Chase's Mills, it too is "A simple place where the past is always present."

One summer on our way to the cabin, we attended a Campus Crusade Lay Institute at Lake Junaluska. Jim's seminar leader, Frank Barker divided the group into twos. Using *The Four Laws*, they role-played how to witness to others. Jim's partner Bob was an endearing backwoods kind of guy. Frank announced that during the week they would take a field trip. Jim knew what that meant, door-to-door witnessing. "D Day" was a surprise and Jim said in no uncertain terms, "We are going home *now!*" I smiled, said "Okay," and began praying.

Jim told Bob, "You need to find another partner, I am not going. "You have to. My battery is dead," replied Bob. Jim was emphatic, "I'll drive, but I am not getting out of the car."

When they arrived at the assigned neighborhood, Jim tried to use the rain as an excuse, but the rain promptly stopped. They approached two boys playing on a porch. "Our Mom isn't home right now," they said. Bob, not wanting to miss God's appointment, shared with the eldest boy, but the young brother was disruptive. Jim took him aside to distract him, but ended up sharing *The Four Laws*. They both accepted Christ! When their mother came home, she saw the tag on Jim's car and asked, "Who is from Orange County?" Conversation revealed that her brother was a deacon at the same church we attended. The deacon cried when he told Jim he had been praying for his nephews for ten years! After that, Jim was more eager to be used by the Lord to share the Good News.

Changes come with aging. My Jim, so dapper in his Brooks Brothers suit, and yet a man who could build a latrine, began losing his spark. Ever so subtly, he began forgetting the familiar, becoming detached, and in ways out of character. Something was happening to the love of my life. In 1996, our family would face a journey that no one ever wants to experience — Alzheimer's.

Losing someone to an accident or disease that destroys the body is very hard, but it seemed harder to lose him slowly to an illness that steals memories, alters personality, and leaves a family with years of grief. I was totally blind and unprepared for the road that lay ahead.

*"I will lead the blind by ways they have not known, along unfamiliar paths I will guide them"* (Isaiah 42:16).

Before Jim's disease advanced I asked his sister, Janie to come and visit. She is ten years younger than Jim, a nurse, a mother of five children, an artist, a widow, and lives in Montana. Her husband, John was a military chaplain. When he retired he became the Priest at the Bozeman Episcopal Church. After many years, it was good to see Jim and Janie enjoying this special time together.

We were at our great-granddaughter Jordan's first birthday party when Jim disappeared. Grandson Darin and his wife Tracy were late for the party, which proved to be *providential*. They saw Jim walking briskly down the street and brought him back to the house. By the grace of God, he had not wandered in the opposite direction, which had major highway traffic! It was frightening and still brings flashbacks. But God was there.

> "...Do not fear, for I have redeemed you; I have called you by name; You are mine! When you pass through the waters, I will be with you. When you pass through the rivers, they will not overflow you. When you walk through the fire, you will not be scorched; nor will the flame burn you. For I am the LORD your God, the Holy One of Israel, your Savior" (Isaiah 43:1-3).

Jim became increasingly difficult. Sometimes his anger flared when I had to tell him what to do. He would say, "You're not my boss!" I asked myself, "How could a close marriage of so many years end like this?" Jim walked incessantly, hardly sleeping night or day. Door locks had to be changed to prevent him from wandering. I wanted to care for him at home, but I had come to the end of my strength.

In May 2002, I chose a facility designed specifically for those with Alzheimer's. John helped me move familiar furniture and belongings from home into his room. Leaving him was the most awful step on this journey. The doctor said, "He needs to adjust; I suggest you not come back for two weeks." These two weeks were heart wrenching for me, but he was safe and well cared for at Arden Courts.

Two weeks later when I entered his room; he grinned and said, "You're here! There *IS* a God in Heaven!" We spent the next three years enjoying each other, walking indoors and out, laughing, singing, and reading Scripture. The friction ended as he didn't see me as his "boss" anymore. Now others were directing him and caring for his needs, so we could enjoy just being together.

One day in 2005, Jim was especially alert. He spoke my name for the first time in years. But within hours, he could not even be awakened. I moved into his room to stay with him. For seven days he never woke up. We prayed, played Christian music, and dampened his mouth with ice. As the end drew near, our daughters, their husbands, grandson Jimmy and I gathered around his bed. As we clung to each other, Dede and Ken sang Jim's favorite hymns. Then he was gone. Yet in reality, he'd been leaving us for ten years.

We sang the Doxology and the first words that came to me were:

> *"The Lord giveth, and the Lord taketh away. Blessed be the name of the Lord"* (Job 1:21).

163

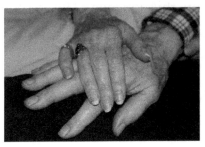 We had been married almost fifty-five years. Life would be different now, but I knew we would be united again in heaven. My loved one with whom I shared everything in life was gone. "The light of our fellowship was extinguished." My best friend, my protector, was not at my side. We had complemented each other; where one was weak, the other was strong. "There is a treasure in the darkness. God wants me to shine so that the light of Jesus may be revealed in me."

John and I went to the funeral home to choose an urn for Jim's ashes, but nothing seemed suitable. John said, "They just don't look like Dad." Then with a grin, "Why not bury his ashes in a Brooks Brothers box?" I agreed…very suitable.

In that unique coffer, we buried his ashes in the woods near our cabin. Mommy's ashes were already there. We had begun our own little private cemetery, reading Psalm 17:15 at his gravesite:

*"And when I awake in heaven, I will be fully satisfied, for I shall see You face-to-face" (Psalm 17:15).*

Our North Carolina pastor, Bud Smythe read Jim's favorite verse:

*"But we have this treasure in jars of clay to show that this all-surpassing power is from God and not from us. We are hard pressed on every side, but not crushed; perplexed, but not in despair; persecuted, but not abandoned; struck down, but not destroyed. We always carry around in our body the death of Jesus, so that the life of Jesus may also be revealed in our body"* (II Corinthians 4:7-10).

I began the adjustment of being a widow. My natural inclination was to withdraw — but instead I saw Jim as my heavenly cheerleader, wanting me to be strong, and involved with others.

I found solace in being with my Christian friends. God designed us to live in community and in hard times it is vital to be connected with the body of Christ...I had the support of godly women from Marty's Bible class, church members, Crusade staff and my newer "Saucer Sisters." The Lord brought women into my life who were also dealing with their husband's Alzheimer's. Helping them gave me new purpose.

But no relationship or endeavor in life would ever replace my love, my hero, Jim.

*To my love on our 50th wedding Anniversary*

*It seems like yesterday when on a July evening in Darien Connecticut, I saw you "across a crowded room." You were tall, dark, and handsome just as I always knew my prince would be. You were so outgoing (sparky sanguine I was to learn later.) But I was such a shy thing, that your savoir-faire frightened me. Even so, we were drawn to each other, but it wasn't until a year later that our whirlwind courtship began.*

*There are many things that I love and admire about you... your fabulous smile, your twinkling eyes, your contagious laugh, and you are always the gentleman and treat me like a lady. You are so considerate, respectful, and generous…giving to, and helping others. You are an encourager, and a great raconteur. You and I did not have secrets, we were able to be open with each other, and I always knew you loved me deeply. You have loved your children and grandchildren. You honored your parents and I am grateful for how you loved and respected C.B. and Marjorie.*

*You were so amenable when I dragged you off to Florida. You have been supportive of my "projects." We have been a team, working side-by-side renovating houses from Larchmont to North Carolina. We were a writing team…letters to the Editor, Bible lessons, and your Adirondack story. We were a Republican duo as our love and concern for our country propelled us into politics.*

*Then the greatest joy was when you surrendered your heart and will to Jesus Christ in 1970. Then we became a new team; ministering to others, giving our testimonies, teaching about marriage, showing the Jesus film in Antigua. What a thrill to hear you preach at Circle Community Church!*

*Yes, we had some rough times but those times were profitable for pruning and our growth. We worked through them together as a three-way team trusting the Lord.*

*Even though in 1948 we didn't know Him, I thank God for bringing us together. I never wanted to be a player on anyone else's team. You have been the only man I have ever loved! Thank you for 50 great years my love!*

*Pug*

# 24

# Sentimental Journey

In 2000, we surprised Margie, Dede, and John with their Christmas gift, a "Sentimental Journey" to New York, taking them to places of family history. In Manhattan they saw where Jim and I had our first date, the church where we were married, and the Plaza where our reception was held.

We took a carriage ride in Central Park, saw the hospital where they were born. Later we had lunch with Jim Arrington who couldn't wait to see "his grown up Mivy" and our other two children. Our last stop was at Peter Cooper Village to see the apartment building where we lived as newlyweds. Our day ended by taking an early evening Circle Line Cruise around Manhattan. The Statue of Liberty was silhouetted behind the setting sun as lights began to flicker all over the city.

The next day we drove to Riverdale, toured the house where I grew up and picnicked by the pond. Then to my father's grave at Scarborough's Sleepy Hollow Cemetery. I read aloud a tribute to him:

> *The five of us are standing here today, Daddy, to pay a tribute to you because we all owe you so much. Where would I be if you and Mommy had not chosen me in 1931?*
>
> *You gave me your name, a family, a home, acceptance, protection, and your incredible generosity. You gave me guidance with freedom. You spent time with me...algebra tutoring, crossword puzzles, Sunday visits to the Bronx Zoo. You provided every material need or want. You passed on to me a love for everything French. You gave me exceptional educational opportunities.*
>
> *When I was older, we had lunches at the Columbia Club, football games, theater tickets, and you opened your arms to the man I chose to marry. You gave us a spectacular wedding and furnished our first home. You were a fun and attentive grandfather. Most of all, you*

*gave this little insecure shy girl the deep assurance of your love.*

*I regret not expressing my gratitude openly and more often. Do young people ever realize until they are grown, how much parents give of themselves and their resources? Daddy, I wish you knew this family standing here today. Thank you for the heritage you passed on to us. You were the most wonderful father a girl could ever have. Did you know that, Daddy?*

*We miss sharing life's events with you. The Spencer name has gone on for generations because of the loving, strong, and generous man you were. We pay tribute to you today and also to the Lord Who was behind the scenes placing me into this family. Thank You, Lord.*

*Thank you, Daddy*

*"I will pour out my spirit on your offspring and my blessings on your descendants"* (Isaiah 44:3).

In Woodbury Connecticut, we saw homes and gravesites of the Locke and Stoddard ancestors. Later we drove to the Tokeneke Club in Darien where Jim and I had first danced. Jim and I stood on the balcony and sang a few verses of "Some Enchanted Evening". After touring Jim's boyhood home in Rye, he showed us the home of his closest friend Val Ely, and his neighborhood friend, Barbara Pierce Bush. We ended the trip at our first family house in Larchmont. It was a journey that gave our children a new understanding of us and their heritage.

**Our family at the Larchmont house**

Jim and my stepmother, Irene, had not always seen eye to eye. Seeing a change in him she said, "If Christ can change Jim Locke, then He can do anything." Soon after he gave her *The Four Laws* booklet, she trusted Christ as her own Lord.

At her death, she generously gave me many treasured Riverdale heirlooms—things that held my childhood memories. I rejoiced at her memorial. She planned every detail...the Scriptures to be read, the hymns to be sung, the pastor's message—all gave the glory to God! Another life changed.

**Irene Spencer**

# 25

## *Conclusion*

## The Providence of God

God's *providence* is His almighty power to uphold everything in this world that comes to us not by chance but from His loving hand. He is sovereign; everything is under His control.

> *"He chose us in Him before the foundation of the world...in love He predestined us for adoption as sons through Christ according to the purpose of His will....in Him we have redemption"* (Ephesians 1:4-7).

I don't see coincidences, chance, or haphazard events. My mistakes and sins can be recycled into something good by the power of the Holy Spirit.

♥ A remark at a tea party rescued me and placed me in a new family.

♥ God chose a specific family which would provide a backdrop for His specific purposes.

♥ He gave me a friend who spoke the Lord's Prayer.

♥ When faced with the fear of war, He tugged at my heart to offer up a childlike prayer.

♥ In times of separation, hymns that told of Christ and His salvation played in my mind.

♥ God brought me a husband; He had chosen us both, and by His providence we married.

♥ We chose a church but He chose a godly minister to share the gospel.

♥ He planted a variety of seeds on my path and watered them to bring forth fruit.

♥ My chronic discontent didn't bring us to Florida. God had a plan for a specific location.

♥ Returning to New York from Florida, He took us on a detour to a new job.

♥ Attempts to relocate were rejected because God's unfolding plan was Winter Park.

♥ My *if only* mindset almost cost me my husband; God used two moving cars to keep us together.

♥ A minister's convicting words: "Are you a witch?" brought assurance that He was there.

♥ He gave me a desire to find my sister and used Miss Sykes to intervene for a reunion.

♥ When I had enough of my self-centeredness, God used a travel agent to lead me to a Bible class. The Four Laws revealed my real need was Christ.

*"He lifted me out of the slimy pit, out of the mud and mire; He set my feet on a rock and gave me a firm place to stand. He put a new song in my mouth, a hymn of praise*

*to our God. Many will see...put their trust in the LORD"*
(Psalm 40:2-3).

I am grateful for the Spirit-filled teaching I received from some of the finest Bible scholars in the country. The most important life-changing principle I learned was how to walk in the power of the Holy Spirit. I cannot live the Christian life; only Christ can live it in and through me as I yield to Him, moment by moment. By exchanging my weakness for His power, there will be spiritual growth, an increasing love of Christ, and victorious living. This is the message I want to live by and pass on. My prayer for all my loved ones is to live Spirit-controlled lives.

> *I pray that you will begin to understand how incredibly great His power is to help those who believe Him. It is that same mighty (resurrection) power that raised Christ from the dead...far, far greater than any king or ruler or dictator or leader* (Ephesians 1:19-21).

God has given me a long life and time to be a witness to our family. I have told this story for our daughter Margie and her husband Bill, our daughter Dede and her husband Ken, our son John and his wife Jaymee—for our grandchildren, Darin and Tracy, Ryan and Kimberly, Jim and Tina, Lisa and David, Chelsea, Spencer—our great-grandchildren Jordan and Samuel—Janie's family—and for my sister Shirley and her family.

*"We will tell the next generation the praiseworthy deeds of
the LORD, His power and the wonders He has done...even
the children yet to be born, and they in turn would tell their
children. Then they would put their trust in God"*
(Psalm 78:4, 6-7).

He chose me for Himself, and led the Spencer's to
choose me..."Twice Chosen."

I stand in His presence amazed at what the hand of the
Lord has done!

This is *His* story. To Him be the glory!

# ABOUT THE AUTHOR

Nina Spencer was born and raised in New York. She married Jim Locke, and in 1957, moved their family of three children to Winter Park, Florida. She and Jim were a political team beginning at the precinct level. Nina was elected Republican State Committee Woman, Delegate to the National Convention, and served on the Governor's Advisory Board. While attending a Bible class in 1969, Nina gave her life to Christ. As a couple they were involved in their church, Campus Crusade for Christ, and the Navigators. She has given her testimony at numerous Christian Women's Clubs. Nina was widowed in 2005.